4.18

# What Should Be Done About Illegal Immigration?

David M. Haugen

ReferencePoint
Press®

San Diego, CA

**About the Author**

David M. Haugen is a film and English instructor at Ohio University. He also writes and edits books for publishers of educational reference materials.

**For more information, contact:**
ReferencePoint Press, Inc.
PO Box 27779
San Diego, CA 92198
www. ReferencePointPress.com

**Picture Credits**

Cover: iStockphoto/Juanmonino
 5: John Moore/Getty Images News/Getty Images
11: John Moore/Getty Images News/Getty Images
14: John Moore/Getty Images News/Getty Images
17: John Moore/Getty Images News/Getty Images
20: John Moore/Getty Images News/Getty Images
27: Alex Wong/Getty Images News/Getty Images
29: Ethan Miller/Getty Images News/Getty Images
32: Scott Olson/Getty Images News/Getty Images
34: David McNew/Getty Images News/Getty Images
40: Chip Somodevilla/Getty Images News/Getty Images
43: John Moore/Getty Images News/Getty Images
47: Spencer Platt/Getty Images News/Getty Images
50: John Moore/Getty Images News/Getty Images
55: oranhall/Depositphotos.com
56: Chip Somodevilla/Getty Images News/Getty Images
64: Scott Olson/Getty Images News/Getty Images

LIBRARY OF CONGRESS CATALOGING-IN-PUBLICATION DATA

Names: Haugen, David M., 1976–
Title: What should be done about illegal immigration? / by David M. Haugen.
Description: San Diego, CA : ReferencePoint Press, Inc., 2017. | Series: Issues in society | Audience: Grade 9 to 12. | Includes bibliographical references and index.
Identifiers: | ISBN 9781682821022 (eBook) | ISBN 9781682820995 (hardback)
 Subjects: LCSH: Illegal Immigration--Juvenile literature.

# CONTENTS

# "The Price of the American Dream"

Thirty-two-year-old Armando Ibanez was born in Mexico but now resides as an undocumented worker in the United States. In 2000, at age eighteen, Ibanez crossed the southern US border and took up residence in California, one of many states with large enough Hispanic communities to hide the multitude of illegals of similar backgrounds and ethnicities. His mother and two younger siblings had fled hunger and poverty in Mexico and sneaked across the border the year before. Ibanez remembers the hardships that drove his family to abandon his homeland: "Not having food to eat every day and seeing your mother struggling—seeing your mother struggling to provide food, that's one of the sad memories I have from Mexico."[1]

Telling his story—and the story of countless other illegal immigrants—to CBS News, Ibanez explains how life changed after crossing the border, how the dread of going hungry and simply surviving has been replaced with the worry of being caught. "In general, I think you have to live in fear of being separated from your family any time, any moment," Ibanez states. "We want to stay together. Knowing that's not for sure makes me feel frustrated. It makes me feel frustrated because my life can change any second. . . . I think the price of the American dream is living afraid."[2]

## Opposing Views on What Illegal Immigrants Deserve

Those who champion the rights of illegal immigrants insist that people like Ibanez should not have to live in fear in a country that boasts of being a shelter for the world's poor and downtrodden. They argue that the American dream is what draws immigrants to the nation, promising freedom from oppression and the ability—through hard work—to better one's position or to make an entirely new life. "America forged its identity on the promise that opportunity comes to those who work hard, play by the rules and contribute their fair share to the success of our nation," says Representative Xavier Becerra of California. "We don't ask immigrants who come to this country hopeful and determined to give us their best and then deny them the opportunity to be equal partners in pursuit of life, liberty and happiness."[3] Becerra, like many Americans, pushes for legislation to make illegal immigrants into citizens so that they do not have to live in fear of their families being torn apart or their lives being upended.

However, hard work and residency are not the requirements for citizenship in the United States. Many who immigrate to America do so legally, following a time-consuming process that requires them essentially to wait in line and adhere to certain rules to reach the goal of citizenship. "Illegal immigrants, in their arrogance, have shown they believe our immigration rules do not apply to them," says David Benkof, a senior analyst with the Daily Caller. "They have jumped

> "I think you have to live in fear of being separated from your family any time, any moment. . . . I think the price of the American dream is living afraid."[2]
>
> —Armando Ibanez, an illegal immigrant living in California.

Central American women and children who illegally crossed the US-Mexico border in 2014 await transport to a federal processing center in Texas. Hunger and lack of opportunity (and in some cases, violence) lead millions to seek a new life in the United States.

the line—basically stealing a chance at a better life from millions of people around the world who would like to live in America."[4] According to Benkof and others, illegal immigrants do not deserve a reward for their behavior, and they have no right to ask for favors or expect the nation to excuse their criminal act. As Judy Lacey, a letter writer to Arizona's *Lake Havasu News-Herald*, stated bluntly, "Those who enter our country illegally expect to be handed a free pass, simply take jobs to which they know they are not legally entitled, and still have the gall to complain that America is not doing enough for them."[5] Many who express this kind of frustration and anger believe the government should follow its legal statutes and deport these lawbreakers as quickly as possible.

## The Difficulty of Creating a Just Immigration Policy

Granting citizenship or following through on deportation are just two of the remedies that are discussed in the numerous debates that circulate around the topic of illegal immigration. Many of these discussions focus on what various politicians or concerned citizens believe is right for the nation, such as securing borders and defining who can and cannot partake in the American dream. Some observers have noted that these debates often ignore the experiences, hardships, and contributions of the individuals and families who are at their center. Offering a plea for all the illegals who have sought shelter in the United States but are too often treated as numbers or stereotypes, Ibanez says, "We just want to be acknowledged in this society as human beings. I just want to be acknowledged that I exist."[6] Many illegals feel trapped in their situation—even if it is of their own making.

Devising policy that is both fair and humane has never been easy in the history of America's dealings with its illegal immigrant population. Proposed strategies involve economic considerations, logistical planning, and ethical deliberation. It is not only a weighing of pros against cons but also a careful assessing of what America stands for and how it wishes to be seen in the global community. America has always been a beacon for immigrants, yet it has also always been a nation that respects the rule of law. The challenge of appeasing these two aspects of the nation's identity is why illegal immigration has remained the subject of heated debate for decades.

# CHAPTER 1

# What Are the Facts?

According to the US Citizenship and Immigration Services (USCIS), in 2014 more than 1 million individuals from foreign countries were given lawful permanent resident status in the United States. A lawful permanent resident is one to whom the government has granted the right to live and work in the United States. More than two-thirds of these new immigrants came from Asia and the Americas (Canada, Mexico, and various Caribbean islands). Many of these will wait out the five-year period to become naturalized US citizens (three years if the individual is a spouse of a US citizen; almost immediately for some in the US armed services). Of those whose wait period expired in 2014, roughly 653,000 earned naturalization that year.

The US government places a cap of 675,000 permanent immigrants allowed into the country each year (with exceptions for close family members), which is why many people who apply for lawful permanent resident status do not achieve it. Some are turned away; others are put on lists to await the opportunity in subsequent years. Whether an individual receives a Permanent Resident Card (commonly known as a green card) depends on various criteria. For instance, the USCIS doles out only a specific number of green cards to immigrants from each country in the world. Countries with fewer immigrants in the United States get a larger share of green cards. The United States also prefers individuals with university degrees or job skills that are in demand; in contrast, it hands out only five thousand green cards worldwide to lower-skilled workers, according to the American Immigration Council.

## The Illegal Population

Because obtaining a green card can be a difficult—and even costly—process, numerous immigrants choose to enter the United States illegally each year. The USCIS estimates that a total of 1.3 million immigrants came to the country in 2014, and 1 million of those became lawful permanent residents. This means that nearly 300,000 of those crossed US borders illegally. The number of illegal entries is uncertain, however, and statistics vary from one count to another. According to the Migration Policy Institute (using 2013 data gathered by the US Census Bureau), 71 percent of the illegal population come from Mexico and Central America (56 percent from Mexico alone). Another 14 percent come from Asia. The remainder arrive from South America, Europe, Africa, and the Caribbean, in that order. The American Immigration Council (using data from a 2010 Pew Research Center study) reports that illegal immigrants make up more than one-fourth of the total immigrant population in the United States. With data taken from a 2012 US Department of Homeland Security (DHS) survey, the American Immigration Council also notes that 42 percent of the illegal population arrived after 2000 and more than 83 percent after 1990.

> "Tackling [illegal immigration] effectively involves overcoming a common misperception that unauthorized immigrants consist primarily of barely literate, single young men who have recently crossed the southern border and live solitary lives disconnected from U.S. society."[7]
>
> —American Immigration Council, a Washington, DC–based nonprofit research organization.

As the numbers suggest, undocumented immigrants are not a unified group, and some experts insist that plans to deal with illegal immigration must accurately portray the population at hand. As the American Immigration Council asserts, "Tackling this issue effectively involves overcoming a common misperception that unauthorized immigrants consist primarily of barely literate, single young men who have recently crossed the southern border and live solitary lives disconnected from U.S. society."[7] According to a 2012 Pew survey, there are 11.7 million illegal immigrants living in the United States (up from 11.2 million in 2010). Sources conflict on this number, but most politicians and commentators refer to it as the accepted baseline. However, few of these experts tend to break down the demographics of this population.

## Illegal Immigrant Demographics and Motivations

Of the more than 11 million illegals that Pew estimated in 2010, 46 percent of the adult immigrants (over age eighteen) have minor children. Minor children accounted for 1 million of the illegal population in that year, while 4.5 million children of undocumented parents were native-born US citizens. According to the DHS survey, 61 percent of illegals are between ages twenty-five and forty-four, and 53 percent are male. Males account for the majority of the younger

# Crossing the US-Mexico Border

Antonio Alarcon was eleven years old when his parents brought him across the Mexican border into America. Although he speaks fondly of eventually starting a new life in New York, he also carries with him the memories of making the dangerous crossing.

I remember that one warm evening when we started walking across the border. The silence of the desert warned us of the danger we faced, and we knew we had to be very careful. My parents advised me not to stray away from them. The minutes passed like hours and we didn't seem to be getting anywhere.

We quickly ran out of water and food. The only thing we found was an irrigation canal in the middle of the desert. We could hear barking dogs and the mooing of cows, as if there was a farm nearby. Everybody started to fill his or her bottles with water from that river. Our only filter was a piece of cloth that my dad ripped off from his shirt. When we were drinking it, we could feel and taste the earth. We did not care though; all we wanted was to quench our thirst.

Three days later, we finally arrived in Arizona. By the time we arrived, many of us had our feet full of sores, and many of us were also dehydrated. From Arizona, we traveled to Los Angeles by car—nine people squeezed into a car meant for four. Upon arriving to Los Angeles, we caught a flight to New York, which became my new home.

Antonio Alarcon, "My Immigration Story," FWD.us, April 2, 2014. www.fwd.us.

population (ages eighteen to thirty-four), but females make up the majority of those over age forty-five. The Migration Policy Institute reveals that 24 percent of undocumented adults possess a high school diploma or a general equivalency diploma; 13 percent have an advanced or professional degree. Because illegal immigrants do not have the same job opportunities as citizens, many are employed in low-skilled occupations. However, the Migration Policy Institute found undocumented workers in education management, entertainment, and the sciences. In addition, 31 percent are homeowners, 32 percent lived at or above 200 percent of the poverty level (32 percent lived below the poverty level), and 63 percent lacked health insurance.

> "Economic incentives alone typically do not induce otherwise law-abiding people to violate the law. And, my study shows that unauthorized migrants are no different."[8]
>
> —Emily Ryo, a law professor at the University of Southern California.

The levels of education and income may be surprising to some; so, too, may be the reasons illegals seek a new life in the United States. Research published in the *American Sociological Review* in August 2013 reveals the motivations behind US border crossings. That research compared the beliefs of Mexicans who intended to migrate against the beliefs of those who did not. University of Southern California law professor Emily Ryo does not discount the overwhelming argument that undocumented workers come to the United States because of job opportunities. She acknowledges that this is the main draw. "But this conventional story misses a critical point," Ryo contends, "because economic incentives alone typically do not induce otherwise law-abiding people to violate the law. And, my study shows that unauthorized migrants are no different."[8]

Ryo found that those who intended to migrate also were influenced by the fact that they had family members or friends who had already attempted or succeeded in crossing the border. Following in their footsteps, Ryo argues, has become a culturally ingrained practice. "Communities with a long history and high prevalence of out-migration might have a culture of migration and, for many young men, migration can be seen as a rite of passage,"[9] she states. Furthermore, Ryo explains that many illegal immigrants from Mexico have no moral qualms about attempting to cross. She found that "respondents who intend to migrate illegally are more likely to think that 'the U.S. government has no right to limit immigration' and 'Mexicans have a right to be in the United States' without the U.S. government's permission."[10] Thus, Ryo claims that many illegals simply disregard US immigration laws because they do not believe in them and that this justification guides border crossers in choosing to leave lives of poverty in their home communities.

## Crossing the Border

Because Mexicans make up the largest share of illegal entrants each year, the southern US border is the most common entry point for illegal immigration. Illegals from Central America also make their way through Mexico to use this point of entry, as do

A suspected smuggler paddles undocumented Salvadoran immigrants across the Rio Grande into the United States. Desperate to cross the border, illegal immigrants pay smugglers to ferry them on rafts or guide them on long, dangerous treks across the desert.

# The Immigration and Nationality Act

While immigration policy continues to be shaped by several factors—including recent executive action by President Barack Obama—the core legislation was codified in 1952 under the McCarran-Walter Act, more commonly known as the Immigration and Nationality Act. The act brought together several different codes into one section of US law. It did away with racial preferences of past laws (such as could be found in a 1790 law, in which "free white persons" of "good moral character" were privileged for naturalization). Additionally, it established nationality quotas based on the percentage of different ethnicities living in the United States. The act has been amended several times over the years. It now includes definitions and procedures relating to topics such as proper documentation, work permits, naturalization, and deportation. The law was amended significantly by the Immigration and Nationality Act of 1965 (also known as the Hart-Celler Act), which dispensed with quotas in favor of a system that incorporated preferences for skilled workers and limited immigration from various parts of the world. It also expanded the total number of legal immigrants to seven hundred thousand per year.

Many see the Immigration and Nationality Act as a useful way to maintain some control over who is admitted to the United States and who is eligible for naturalization. Others believe the policy is dated. They view it as racially elitist, especially given that in 1965, America was 85 percent (non-Hispanic) white, while by 2013 that percentage had fallen to 63 and will decrease to 50 percent by 2042, according to US census projections.

others from the Caribbean and more distant places such as India and Africa. Since the Rio Grande defines much of the border between Mexico and Texas, immigrants trying this route often look for shallow spots to cross. "Others pay smugglers to ferry them on rafts, boats, even jet skis. They carry their clothes on their heads and put important paperwork in Ziploc bags,"[11] Edgar Sandoval writes in a *New York Daily News* article. Those who attempt to cross through the deserts and mesas that make up the borders with California, Arizona, and New Mexico face long walks through harsh climates. Some might pay smugglers to hide them in vans or trucks and drive them through border crossing checkpoints.

Other illegal immigrants choose different paths into the United States. Travelers from the Dominican Republic and Haiti often sail to Puerto Rico or Florida. Some from Asia or the Pacific island nations are smuggled aboard ships that dock on the West Coast. A large portion of illegal immigrants from all over the world come to America on legal visas as students, visitors, or workers and simply overstay their visit, blending into communities in hopes of avoiding detection. The *Wall Street Journal* reported in April 2013 that about 40 percent of illegals in the United States possess expired visas. Reporter Sara Murray notes:

> Little is known about the demographics of the so-called overstayer population, but some studies suggest they tend to be better educated and more fluent in English than those who crossed the border illegally. They also are more likely to hail from European, Asian and African countries. . . . Studies show that over the past decade the number of new arrivals overstaying their visas has fallen sharply, likely due in large part to stringent security measures put in place after the Sept. 11, 2001, terrorist attacks.[12]

Once illegals cross the southern border or otherwise arrive in the United States, they find communities in which to live. For example, many Mexican border crossers choose residency in states and cities with large Hispanic populations. According to the Migration Policy Institute, "In 2014, the top five U.S. states by number of immigrants were California (10.5 million), Texas and New York (4.5 million each), Florida (4 million), and New Jersey (2 million)."[13] While these numbers include all immigrants, a large portion of them are illegal immigrants. Illegal immigrants further integrate themselves into these communities by finding jobs to support themselves and their families. Some use fake work documents or hijacked Social Security numbers that they hope—or assume—their employers will not check. Others find jobs in sectors of the economy—such as agriculture, housekeeping, or the textile trade—where they might be paid under the table by employers who rely on cheap labor. For these reasons, some illegals pay taxes, but some do not. However, holding down a job and raising a family help these individuals feel more rooted in their new home.

## Deterring Illegals at the Border

Keeping illegal immigration from getting rooted in the United States is a difficult task for authorities. The DHS is the cabinet-level division that oversees illegal immigration matters. US Customs and Border Protection (CBP), one of its agencies, maintains watch over America's borders and its points of entry. CBP officers interview anyone seeking proper entry to the country and catch and detain others who cross the borders unlawfully. In short, the CBP states that in carrying out his or her job, "a CBP officer may question, under oath, any person coming into the United States to determine his or her admissibility."[14]

*A US Customs and Border Protection officer takes down information after detaining an illegal border crosser in 2015. Some CBP officers have been accused of abusing undocumented immigrants, but others have helped immigrants victimized by smugglers.*

Unfortunately, the CBP has also been accused of abusing immigrants. In 2016, for example, the American Civil Liberties Union (ACLU) filed a complaint against several officers for abuses that included arbitrary strip searches and unlawful detainment of legal permanent residents. "They can hurl unfounded allegations at someone, and they don't need to provide evidence of their claim," ACLU field organizer Cynthia Pompa told CNN. "They can act as a judge. They can act as a jury. They can act as a deporter. And it all goes unchecked."[15] Still, the majority of CBP officers feel they are just doing a difficult job in challenging circumstances and environments and must be on guard against unscrupulous or violent people.

Jim Glennon, a retired police lieutenant from Illinois, defends his fellow law enforcement officers in the CBP by stressing the dangers they face. "It seems like 99.9 percent of the time, the media line is that 99.9 percent of the people crossing our southern border are just poor innocents looking for work and a meager wage," Glennon says. "Evaluated in the most simplistic terms, this is of course, partly true. But the more complex reality isn't that simple or sanitary." He goes on to discuss the Mexican gangs and smugglers that bring violence to the border. Coupled with the day-to-day rescues of immigrants in peril and the difficulties in pursuits, the violence only makes the job more dangerous; and Glennon invites readers to "check out the statistics and see how many of our Border Patrol Agents have been killed in the line of duty over the past 20+ years: car accidents, pursuit fatalities, heat stroke, heart attacks, drowning, vehicular homicide, and murder."[16]

## Roundups and Deportation

While the CBP deters or catches immigrants violating points of entry, US Immigration and Customs Enforcement (ICE) is tasked with hunting down and removing illegal immigrants once they establish themselves within the nation. Formed in the wake of the September 11, 2001, terrorist attacks, ICE and its parent, the DHS, are relatively new organizations. Both are concerned with terrorist threats on American soil, but they have the added

15

responsibility of dealing with the illegal population. Among other duties, ICE is often called on to stage raids on suspected illegal immigrant homes, investigate workplaces that may hire illegal immigrants, enforce codes involving undocumented criminals, and monitor the detention of anyone caught by immigration authorities. In 2015, ICE—with the help of the CBP and local law enforcement—removed 235,413 individuals from the country. Of this total, 69,478 were apprehended in the nation's interior, and 165,935 were nabbed near US borders. Ninety-one percent of interior captures and removals were of convicted criminals (of any offense other than traffic violations), while nearly 46 percent of border area removals were criminals. According to its website, in 2015, ICE "placed increased emphasis and focus on the removal of convicted felons and other public safety threats over non-criminals."[17] Because ICE has targeted its enforcement on criminals, the overall number of deportations is lower than in previous years. "ICE is not going to pursue anyone unless they can really justify the cause for it,"[18] remarks Janice Kephart, the former national security director at the Center for Immigration Studies.

> "ICE is not going to pursue anyone unless they can really justify the cause for it."[18]
>
> —Janice Kephart, the former national security director at the Center for Immigration Studies.

Once captured, detainees may spend time in ICE detention facilities around the country or in one of several state or county jails where the overflow is kept. There, they wait until tried in the courts or deported. Amnesty International published a fifty-one-page report in 2009, citing many abuses within this detention and deportation system. For example, the organization claims not every undocumented immigrant is notified that they have rights that may ultimately allow them to stay in the United States. Some are shipped to remote locations, where legal assistance may be out of easy reach and contact with family members on either side of the border is not provided. Of the facilities themselves, Amnesty International claims that in some cases "conditions of detention . . . do not meet either international human rights standards or ICE guidelines."[19]

*A guard at an ICE detention facility in California escorts an immigrant detainee to his cell. Thousands of detainees awaiting decisions on their future are housed in detention centers or jails around the country.*

## An Uncertain Future

Undocumented immigrants who have not been uncovered by ICE live with the fear that authorities might eventually find them during a workplace raid, from an anonymous tip, or through household accounts or even their children's school records. Because they do not wish to risk being caught, they may forgo seeing a doctor if they are sick (or if their child is sick). They may be exploited by landlords or employers because they fear seeking legal help for possible injustices. "The undocumented are in a subclass below those at the bottom of the social pyramid because they do not possess citizenship," writes Jean-Claude Velasquez, a Colombian-born Stony

Brook University student who lived as an illegal but has since become naturalized. "Without citizenship, life in the United States is extremely limited and bleak."[20] Many wait and hope that the nation will look kindly on those who have spent much of their lives living and working in America and give them a way to achieve citizenship.

> "The undocumented are in a subclass below those at the bottom of the social pyramid because they do not possess citizenship."[20]
>
> —Jean-Claude Velasquez, a university student and former undocumented immigrant.

However, polls continue to show that a majority of Americans favor political policies to gain control of the country's borders rather than granting a pathway to citizenship for undocumented immigrants. Other surveys support claims that US citizens are both wary and concerned about illegal immigration. For example, an August 2014 Reuters poll found that 70 percent of Americans believe that undocumented immigrants "threaten traditional U.S. beliefs and customs," and 63 percent agree that illegals "place a burden on the economy."[21] In a January 2015 Gallup Poll, 39 percent of Americans said they would like to see all types of immigration into the United States decrease.

Jeff Sessions, a US senator from Alabama and an opponent of any form of amnesty for illegal immigrants, claims, "For decades, the American people have begged and pleaded for a just and lawful system of immigration that serves their interests—but their demands are refused."[22] He believes Congress and several presidential administrations have pressed their own agendas that offer to forgive those undocumented immigrants already in the United States and encourage more to come. Whether the government is refusing to acknowledge the will of the people or whether the will of the people is not as unified as Sessions indicates is debatable. Within that debate, though, is the future of America's undocumented population and the possibility of immigration reform.

# Should America Strengthen Disincentives to Hiring Illegal Workers?

Although illegal immigrants might choose to enter the United States for multiple reasons, the primary draw is employment. The roughly half million illegals who cross the southern US border each year are overwhelmingly from Mexico and Central American countries, where poverty is widespread. America appears to be a land of opportunity in which others—friends or family members, perhaps—have started new, more prosperous lives. For example, Mexico's unemployment rate in 2016 was just over 4 percent, but according to the *CIA World Factbook*, underemployment in the country may be as high as 25 percent. Thus, many Mexicans cross the border because they see the promise of a better future—for themselves and their loved ones—that is not apparent in their homeland. The same motivations inspire immigrants from Asia, South America, and other regions.

According to organizations such as the Pew Research Center and the Center for Immigration Studies, illegal immigrants in the United States tend to find jobs in select fields. In a 2009 report, the Center for Immigration Studies found that immigrants (both legal and illegal) held a majority in the US workforce in four occupations: plasterers and stucco masons (56 percent), agricultural product graders and sorters (54 percent), miscellaneous personal appearance workers (such as at hair and nail salons; 53 percent), and tailors, sewers, and dressmakers (51 percent). According to the report, these occupations make up less than 1 percent of the US workforce. Overall, though, undocumented immigrants constitute just over 5 percent of the total US workforce, according to a 2014 Pew study. In a broader study of illegal immigrants in America in 2009, the Pew Research Center found that the occupations with the highest percentage of illegals (over 10 percent) included broad categories such as farming (25 percent); building, groundskeeping, and maintenance (19 percent); construction (17 percent); and food preparation and serving (12 percent). The Center for Immigration

*A migrant farmworker from Mexico harvests zucchini in Colorado. Undocumented immigrants have a strong presence in low-skill, low-pay jobs in farming, building maintenance, groundskeeping, construction, and food preparation.*

Studies states that occupations such as these are often erroneously termed "jobs Americans won't do," but even if that charge is inaccurate, these jobs are typically low skilled and low paying, which gives immigrants an opening into these fields.

## Why Do Employers Hire Illegal Immigrants?

Illegal immigrants flock to—or at least end up in—these jobs because employers in these fields need laborers and because paying lower wages to undocumented immigrants is cheaper than paying US workers to do the same jobs. In some cases employers pay their illegal workers in cash so that they can keep them off company books. Even if the worker is on the official company payroll, his or her wages still may be lower. According to the Bureau of Labor Statistics, in 2014 the median weekly earnings of all foreign-born workers was $664, while native-born workers earned $820 for comparable work.

In addition to saving money, companies find other reasons to use the undocumented immigrant labor pool. In a 2014 article for Bloomberg View, reporter Francis Wilkinson tells of a friend who hires illegals for a few reasons: They are often helpful at recruiting other illegals, they are self-policing—meaning they make sure workers are pulling their own weight—and they do not take their employment lightly. In contrast, Wilkinson says his employer friend "found many of the Americans he has hired over the years to be unreliable and unwilling to work hard."[23] For this reason, the employer says he pays immigrant workers the same pay as native workers.

Even though it is unlawful to hire undocumented workers, those employers, like Wilkinson's friend, who use them have little motivation to root out these individuals from their workforce. Businesses are supposed to check verification documents presented by each employee when he or she fills out a federal I-9 work-eligibility form, but potential hires have some choice in terms of what documents they are allowed to submit. Employers are not experts in catching forgeries, and because the I-9 is not filed with the government, they are the sole gatekeepers. It is up to employers to inspect each document "to determine if it reasonably appears to be genuine and to relate to the person presenting it,"[24] as the I-9 instructions say. As long as employers are reasonably satisfied, they can move forward with the hire. In fact, the I-9 form warns employers that mistakenly barring an employee may be a form of discrimination. "The federal government does not expect businesses to act like immigration gumshoes," write the editors of the *Oregonian* in a September 2014 opinion piece. "Meanwhile, economic reality provides no incentive for employers to exercise more curiosity than they must."[25]

> "The federal government does not expect businesses to act like immigration gumshoes. Meanwhile, economic reality provides no incentive for employers to exercise more curiosity than they must."[25]
>
> —Editors of the *Oregonian* newspaper.

## Calling Out Companies

The fact that American businesses are either not more diligent in investigating new hires or even willingly hire undocumented

# Businesses Are Routinely Penalized for Hiring Undocumented Workers

The *Wall Street Journal* reported in 2015 that the Obama administration has kept up efforts to penalize companies that knowingly hire undocumented workers.

Broetje Orchards in Washington state, one of the country's largest apple growers, has agreed to pay a $2.25 million fine for hiring illegal immigrants. The fine is one of the largest ever levied against an agricultural concern, according to government officials who announced it Thursday.

The Broetje case, which dragged on for years, highlights the uncertain environment for employers as U.S. immigration policy remains in flux.

Since January 2009, the Obama administration has conducted immigration audits of more than 13,700 employers, mostly in the construction, hospitality, manufacturing and farming sectors. Companies have paid tens of millions of dollars in fines and had to dismiss thousands of workers.

"The Obama administration has eased up on enforcement for immigrant workers and their families, but not against employers," said Tamar Jacoby, president of ImmigrationWorks USA, a network of employers in industries such as hospitality, construction and food processing that hire low-skilled workers. "Audits haven't stopped."

Miriam Jordan, "Washington State Fruit Grower Hit with $2.25 Million Immigration Fine," *Wall Street Journal*, June 4, 2015. www.wsj.com.

workers has angered many US citizens. Some hope to inflame public opinion against companies known for such practices. The Facebook page "List of Companies That Hire Illegal Aliens Instead of Americans" is one example of a grassroots attempt to point fingers at and perhaps shame companies that supposedly cheat Americans out of jobs. The page is an offshoot of the now-defunct website WeHireAliens.com, which invited users to accuse companies—reportedly more than twenty-seven hundred of them—of breaking the law. WeHireAliens.com was founded by Jason Mrochek, who was frustrated with the government's inability to enforce hiring laws. According to a 2007 article in the *Arizona Republic*, WeHireAliens.com gathered and acted on word-of-mouth information. "Mrochek reviews the information to

# Businesses Are Rarely Penalized for Hiring Undocumented Workers

The Center for Immigration Studies claims that in 2015 the government dropped aggressive actions against employers who hire undocumented workers. Largely, this has meant a decrease in audits and raids of suspect companies.

ICE records obtained by the Center indicate that after an initial flurry of activity from 2010 to 2013, even [paperwork] worksite auditing efforts have been curtailed significantly, with a very sharp drop in recent years. The number of audits conducted has fallen from a high of 3,127 in 2013 to 1,320 in 2014. This year, ICE is on track to complete fewer than 500 audits.

Fewer audits means that there have been fewer sanctions against employers. From 2010 to 2014, the number of employers arrested for worksite immigration violations hovered near 200 per year. This year, ICE is on track to arrest fewer than 70 employers.

The amount of fines collected from offending employers also has dropped sharply. In each year from 2011 to 2014, ICE collected more than $8 million in fines from offending employers. This year, ICE is on track to collect less than $5 million in fines.

Jessica Vaughan, "ICE Records Reveal Steep Drop in Worksite Enforcement Since 2013," Center for Immigration Studies, June 2015. www.cis.org.

**VIEWPOINT**

see if it seems credible," the newspaper said. "If he deems the accusations add up to what he calls 'reasonable suspicion,' he goes ahead and posts the company on a list of businesses to boycott and then forwards the information to ICE, the FBI and the Social Security Administration."[26]

The website's last posting was in 2014. However, both the Facebook page and the website attracted their share of heated argument. Some Facebook users accused the page of racism, while the *Arizona Republic* cited Farrell Quinlan, a spokesperson for the Arizona Chamber of Commerce and Industry, as particularly critical of the website. "The virtual vigilantism of this site encourages anonymous informants and the trafficking of whispered innuendo,"[27] Quinlan remarked. The newspaper included statements from some business leaders and employees who claimed that many of the charges were unjust but who could do nothing to stop the outpouring of disparaging comments on the site.

## Federal Efforts to Penalize Businesses That Hire Illegals

The complaints of individuals like Mrochek indicate that some Americans are displeased with existing federal efforts to curb the hiring of illegal immigrants. The 1986 Immigration Reform and Control Act made it unlawful for companies to hire illegal workers. It also spelled out the penalties for doing so. Companies can be fined between $250 and $2,000 for each first offense violation; subsequently hiring illegals can increase the penalty from $2,000 up to $10,000 per employee. Such unlawful acts may also result in the loss of a company's business license and criminal prosecution.

To avoid prosecution, some companies have paid large settlements after being investigated by ICE. In 2012, for example, two Houston businesses—Advanced Containment System Inc. and Champion Window—lost $2 million each after ICE audits found that roughly 44 percent and 60 percent, respectively, of their workforces were composed of illegals. "Each company is forfeiting a substantial amount of money," affirmed Robert Rutt, an ICE special agent in Houston. "It sends a message that these actions—while not criminally prosecuted—still have consequences."[28]

Despite notable settlements, some commentators still claim that the law is difficult to enforce and that employers are not significantly deterred from using undocumented workers. Since they must only show good faith effort in keeping out illegals, few companies are indicted. Those that are often agree to settlements to avoid further criminal penalties. In addition, ICE seems to have become lax in enforcement. In a 2015 article, the Center for Immigration Studies reported that between October 2014 and February 2015, "ICE conducted just 181 workplace audits and brought charges against just 27 employers."[29] This is down from 2013, when 3,000 companies were investigated and 179 employers faced prosecution. With more settlements and fewer criminal penalties, companies that use undocumented workers recognize that getting caught may result in only a financial slap on the wrist.

## An Electronic Work-Eligibility Verification System

In his January 29, 2013, remarks on immigration reform, Barack Obama asserted that if the country really wanted to show its commitment to fair hiring practices, it would have to "stay focused on enforcement," and that "means cracking down more forcefully on businesses that knowingly hire undocumented workers." He went on to say, "To be fair, most businesses want to do the right thing, but a lot of them have a hard time figuring out who's here legally, who's not. So we need to implement a national system that allows businesses to quickly and accurately verify someone's employment status."[30] According to the White House, the president's proposal includes instituting a national database that businesses could use to establish a worker's immigrant status and eligibility to work based on government records. In addition, the proposal calls for the creation of fraud-proof documents that can be used by

> "To be fair, most businesses want to do the right thing, but a lot of them have a hard time figuring out who's here legally, who's not. So we need to implement a national system that allows businesses to quickly and accurately verify someone's employment status."[30]
>
> —Barack Obama, forty-fourth president of the United States.

workers to prove their lawful right to work. Such a program was already in place when Obama made his remarks.

The Basic Pilot/Employment Eligibility Verification Program began in 1997 as a measure to curb illegal immigration. It was initiated as a voluntary program through which employers (with their employees' knowledge) could electronically submit workers' I-9 information to ICE for verification. The program was renamed E-Verify in 2007 when the DHS, in conjunction with the Social Security Administration, took over operation of the program and expanded its use by mandating that all government contractors use the service. Though the system has been in use for many years, it has not been made a legal requirement for other businesses, as Obama's proposal anticipated. Enrollment in E-Verify—though free—is still voluntary for businesses that do not perform federal work.

## The Debate over E-Verify

Proponents of E-Verify cite its ease of use and its growing popularity among businesses. While the Basic Pilot Program took a long time to verify a worker's eligibility, the modern system usually informs employers of that status within twenty-four hours. According to the USCIS, more than six hundred thousand companies use E-Verify, and roughly fifteen hundred more enroll each week. In 2013 a Pulse Opinion Research poll found that 78 percent of Americans supported a mandatory verification system as a means to curb illegal immigration. In the same year, a National Association for the Self-Employed survey reported that six out of ten small businesses supported such a mandatory system. Some states have passed their own legislation mirroring the federal mandate, making it a requirement for state agencies and public universities to use E-Verify. In June 2015 Texas governor Greg Abbott signed such a bill. He explained, "This bill adds appropriate checks on the hiring of individuals not lawfully present in this nation by state

"It will be a lot harder for people to come here illegally for labor if they know that when they get here there will be an effort to verify whether or not they have employment authorization."[32]

—John Morton, former director of ICE.

*In 2011, US secretary of homeland security Janet Napolitano announces newly added features of the E-Verify program. Checking a potential worker's eligibility to legally hold a job in the United States is voluntary in the private sector.*

agencies, incentivizes lawful immigration and assures taxpayers that their hard-earned dollars are being used responsibly."[31]

While Abbott contends that Americans might be pleased with E-Verify's ability to help curb taxpayer spending on illegal immigration and, possibly, welfare benefits that undocumented immigrants can still use, others see different advantages to the program. John Morton, the former director of ICE, spoke of such a system as a deterrent to potential illegal immigrants. Morton told C-SPAN's *Washington Journal* program in March 2011, "It will be a lot harder for people to come here illegally for labor if they know that when they get here there will be an effort to verify whether or not they have employment authorization."[32] In early 2015 the latest versions of a mandatory E-Verify bill were presented separately to both houses of Congress. Representative Lamar Smith, a Texas Republican, touted the bill that he introduced into the House of Representatives as an aid to remedying unemployment among the legal population. "Almost 20 million Americans are unemployed or underemployed," Smith stated. "Meanwhile, seven million people are working in the United States illegally. By expanding the E-Verify system, this bill will ensure that jobs only go to legal workers."[33] Smith referred to the same positive outcome in 2011 when he wrote in an editorial for the *American Spectator*, "E-Verify is a program that helps preserve scarce jobs for U.S. citizens and legal immigrants."[34]

Despite the number of times E-Verify legislation has been introduced to Congress, none has passed into law. Detractors claim E-Verify is easy to outwit with fraudulent documents and that too many lawful employees mistakenly get flagged by the system as ineligible. In a 2015 letter to the editor of the *New York Times*, Gabriel Camacho of the American Friends Service Committee, a Quaker organization advocating social justice, says that "an independent study found that lawful permanent residents were four times more likely—and work-authorized immigrants were 27 times more likely—to receive an erroneous E-Verify determination."[35] Alex Nowrasteh, a policy analyst at the Cato Institute, expands this argument by stating:

> If 150 million American workers were run through E-Verify tomorrow, somewhere between 450,000 and slightly more than 1 million American workers would be notified that if they do not address the problem then they will lose their jobs. Those American [workers] would then have to correct any inconsistencies before the government gave them clearance to be employed full time. That hardly seems fair for these legal workers.[36]

Although Nowrasteh admits that the number of erroneous reports has decreased over time, he insists that placing such a burden on legal workers is unjust.

Furthermore, Nowrasteh states that businesses also incur legal fees from mistaken results because they must hire lawyers to help clear the names of work-eligible employees. He estimates that every employee run through E-Verify costs companies $147 in legal fees because some employees may be mistakenly rejected by the system. Thus, the "free" E-Verify program is not really free, given the prospect of erroneous results. Others point out that innocent, work-eligible employees also end up paying fees to

*Adoption of a system of national ID cards could help identify people in the country illegally, but many people oppose this idea. They fear it would allow the government to track citizens' private transactions such as legal gun purchases.*

lawyers to clear their names. While such an expense may not be detrimental to large companies, small businesses and legal workers may not be able to absorb these costs. Nowrasteh states:

> Other costs will be borne by American taxpayers. The E-Verify mandate passed as part of the Senate's [2013] immigration reform bill would impose around $2.1 billion in government expenditures over the course of a decade. That's in addition to the $1.37 billion for technology upgrades and overhead that the bill mandates. Worse, it would require the hiring of 5,000 enforcement [officers] at a cost of approximately $230 million a year, amounting to nearly $2.3 billion over the first decade of the program.[37]

# Fear and Confusion

Such "hidden" outcomes are rife in the criticisms of E-Verify. In a February 2013 article, Henrik Temp of the American Enterprise Institute says that the adoption of E-Verify will only increase trade in stolen identification. "Indeed, the GAO [Government Accountability Office] has already found that 50% of unauthorized hires slipped through E-Verify for exactly this reason," Temp claims. "Moreover, E-Verify will create a treasure trove for identity hackers, who can find lots of personal information, including Social Security Numbers."[38] Some, like Nowrasteh and Temp, also worry that mandating an E-Verify system will lead to the creation of a national identity card that all citizens will have to carry. A national ID card would contain too much personal info, these opponents complain, allowing the government to keep track of its citizens and potentially monitor legal exchanges—such as the purchase of a gun—that should be private. David Bier furthers the argument by insisting that E-Verify opens the doors to limitless accumulation of personal data. "When legislators and regulators begin to discover the possibilities created by E-Verify," he warns, "the end-product ultimately may be what few people who supported the original version envisioned."[39]

> "E-Verify will create a treasure trove for identity hackers, who can find lots of personal information, including Social Security Numbers."[38]
>
> —Henrik Temp, editorial associate at the American Enterprise Institute.

Whether the E-Verify program will prove a boon or a curse to America's attempts to resolve the issue of undocumented workers is unclear. However, the debate over the program reveals a country deeply divided about the benefits and drawbacks of such a large illegal population. Some segments of the nation seem eager for the help undocumented workers provide, while other segments appear distraught by their unlawful presence. In a CNN commentary, nationally syndicated columnist Ruben Navarrette Jr. suggests America has a schizophrenic attitude toward illegal immigrants. "It starts with the two signs at the border: 'Keep out' and 'Help Wanted.' We all but beg them to work for us, and then too often we abuse and exploit them as if we rue the day they punched in."[40] This contradictory reality has made it difficult for Americans to come to any consensus concerning the treatment of the nation's undocumented workforce.

# Should the United States Build a Wall Along the Border with Mexico?

During an April 2015 speech to business leaders in New Hampshire, Republican presidential nominee Donald Trump made various campaign pledges in hopes of wooing voters in the state's upcoming primary election. When asked by someone in the audience about his stance on border security and immigration policy, Trump candidly indicated that he would finally do what some conservative politicians and pundits have suggested for the past two decades: construct a wall along the southern US border. "I will build the best wall, the biggest, the strongest, not penetrable, they won't be crawling over it, like giving it a little jump and they're over the wall,"[41] Trump remarked. His comments seemed to criticize the ineffectiveness of current barriers that exist along certain access points along the US border with Mexico while promising an enormous wall that could not be breached. Four months later in another New Hampshire appearance, Trump, known for the numerous real estate ventures and buildings that bear his name, said of the proposed wall, "I want it to be so beautiful because maybe someday they're going to call it the Trump wall."[42]

## Conservative Calls to Build a Wall

Trump is not the first to suggest sealing off the entire 1,954-mile-long (3,145 km) southern US border. In his bid for the Republican presidential nomination in 2012, businessman and radio personality Herman Cain said he would authorize construction of a 20-foot-tall (6 m) electrified fence topped with barbed wire with a sign on the Mexican side stating, "It will kill you." Cain told voters gathered at stops in Tennessee that he got the idea after returning from China, where he visited the Great Wall. "It looks pretty sturdy. And that sucker is real high," Cain quipped. "I think we can build one if we want to! We have put a man on the moon, we can

A fence separates the American city of Nogales (in Arizona) and the Mexican city of the same name (in Sonora). Despite the fence, this area is a frequent crossing point for people entering the United States illegally.

build a fence! Now, my fence might be part Great Wall and part electrical technology."[43] Although Cain later said his comments were meant to be humorous, he then reversed course again and acknowledged that a border fence—even possibly electrified—was a good idea.

In July 2014 conservative television commentator Bill O'Reilly referenced another famous wall when he talked about a "dereliction of leadership" in dealing with both immigration and criminal problems along the US-Mexico border. O'Reilly implied that America needed its own version of the Berlin Wall. "Nobody could get through that fence. Nobody. It was a formidable obstacle. The Israelis have done the same thing to keep out terrorism there. We haven't done that on the southern border,"[44] O'Reilly flatly asserted, indicating that this failure was a "mistake" repeated by several presidential administrations.

Even if Cain's "killer fence" was meant in part to be a joke, media sources present at the time noted that his comments were met with cheers in Tennessee. Likewise, Trump's words have evoked whistles and applause from those gathered at his presidential primary rallies. According to an August 2015 Rasmussen Reports survey, 70 percent of likely Republican voters support building a wall along the southern border (while only 17 percent of these voters disagree). Expanded to include all voters, the percentage drops to 51 in favor of a wall (and 37 percent opposed). Even if these voters do not support the exact construction strategies offered by Republican candidates or conservative commentators, the survey results attest to how important and polarizing the problem of border security is to Americans.

## How Much Would a Wall Cost?

When grappling with the details of building a wall or fence along the US-Mexico border, many politicians and experts on both sides immediately discuss the cost of undertaking this extensive and expensive project. The federal government has already spent $2.4 billion on single-layer fencing along 670 miles (1,078 km) of the border. The fencing is not contiguous and covers only high-traffic areas in Arizona, California, New Mexico, and Texas. Its construction and costs were approved under the Secure Fence Act of 2006, a bill that was approved by both houses of Congress and signed into law by President George W. Bush. The following year, though, Congress put a hold on further funding in order to revisit the plan and consider the fence within the broader aims of border security.

According to a Government Accountability Office assessment in 2009, 1 mile (1.6 km) of fencing costs between $2.8 and $3.9 million. This estimate was based on the initial 220-mile (354-km) stretch that covered relatively flat terrain. The cost would rise—perhaps significantly—as the barrier was extended over difficult landscapes that might require drainage or other alterations to permit secure fencing. In addition, much of the land along the border is in private hands, and although the government could enact its eminent domain privilege to seize it, it would still have to compensate the owners, driving costs up even more. In October 2015 CNBC estimated, "The actual cost for the rest of the border wall (roughly 1,300 miles) could be as high as $16 million per mile, with a total price tag of $15 billion to $25 billion."[45] This price tag, CNBC notes, does not include the estimated $750 million per year for maintenance and upkeep.

From 2007 to 2015 the DHS has awarded only $5.9 billion to the Border Security Fencing, Infrastructure, and Technology account. This account is a repository for all funds that are used to pay for fencing, repairs, cameras, roads, and other elements of infrastructure needed to secure the border. How the government will make up the difference in costs to finish the entire fence is the subject of its own debates. However, the Trump campaign argues that if all the other factors associated with illegal immigration—including the costs of criminal arrests and prosecutions, the loss of taxable

*An unmarked US Customs and Border Protection vehicle patrols a section of the US-Mexico border in California that is marked only by a sign. Erecting a fence along the entire boundary between the two countries would likely cost billions of dollars.*

income that could be earned by legal workers, and the welfare programs still available to illegals—were taken into account, the price of a permanent barrier and its upkeep would pale in comparison.

## Who Will Pay for the Proposed Wall?

Tired of waiting for the federal government to act, Arizona decided to arrange its own pool of funds to build a barrier along the Arizona-Mexico border. In 2011 Governor Jan Brewer signed into law a measure that permitted the state to use inmate labor and private contractors to build a wall along the border. The law did not appropriate taxpayer money to fund the project but instead opened up accounts for private donations.

In 2013 the Associated Press reported that Arizona lawmakers admitted that "the state has received just $264,000 for the project, well short of the $2.8 million needed to build the first mile of fencing."[46] Thus, the Arizona plan stalled.

> "I will build the wall and Mexico's going to pay for it and they will be happy to [pay] for it. Because Mexico is making so much money from the United States that that's going to be peanuts."[47]
>
> —Donald Trump, 2016 Republican presidential candidate.

More notably, Trump has insisted that as president, he would get Mexico to pay for the wall. Trump made that claim in April 2015 and has repeated it during other press conferences and voter rallies. For example, in a July 31, 2015, interview with CNN, Trump stated, "I will build the wall and Mexico's going to pay for it and they will be happy to [pay] for it. Because Mexico is making so much money from the United States that that's going to be peanuts."[47] In an undated memo on his campaign website, Trump and his advisers outline a plan for getting Mexico to commit $5 billion to $10 billion for the wall. They would block remittances, which refers to money sent by illegal immigrants to family members back in Mexico. This would be accomplished by requiring financial institutions to have customers prove lawful citizenship or visitation status before sending remittance payments. Much of the money illegals make in the United States (more than $24 billion per year, according to BBVA Research, a banking advisory group) is sent back to relatives in Mexico. This sum, Trump

35

# A Border Wall Will Keep Migrants in Mexico

Reporter Christopher Manion argues that Americans should not be quick to discredit the idea of building a border wall. He insists that a wall will force Mexican migrants to stay in their own country and fix the problems that encourage emigration.

[Mexico's ruling party] and Mexico's lavish insider network of politicians, businessmen, and financiers are one and the same, and their unique partnership has made many Mexican politicians and their favored allies some of the richest men in the world. Meanwhile, the Mexican people have remained impoverished, surrounded daily by a culture of violence, gangs, and bribes. . . .

The wall is only one ingredient in the restoration of the rule of law on both sides of the border. On the American side, legal immigrants and their employers will once more have an above-board, mutually rewarding relationship. But those on the Mexican side will prosper as well: while some enterprising Mexicans will continue to apply for legal entrance into the United States, millions more will stay at home and demand that their own government reform the current system that perpetuates poverty, violence, and crime.

Christopher Manion, "Why the Wall Will Work," Breitbart News Network, April 14, 2016. www .breitbart.com.

and others have argued, substitutes for a welfare system, a safety net that Mexico's government does not provide for its citizens. Because the Mexican government would not want this safety net to disappear, Trump contends, Mexico's leaders will be happy to foot a one-time bill to cover the cost of building a border wall. If this tactic is not enough, the Trump campaign believes other threats—such as canceling visitation visas, increasing visa fees, and raising tariffs—will force Mexico to pay.

In August 2015 a spokesperson for Mexican president Enrique Peña Nieto responded to Trump's assertion by saying, "Of course it's false. It reflects an enormous ignorance for what

Mexico represents, and also the irresponsibility of the candidate who's saying it."[48] When asked about his views on the subject in February 2016, former Mexican president Felipe Calderón said more succinctly, "We are not going to pay any single cent for such a stupid wall! And it's going to be completely useless. The first loser of such a policy would be the United States. If this guy pretends that closing the borders to anywhere either for trade [or]

## A Border Wall Will Keep Migrants in the United States

Douglas Massey, a professor of sociology and public affairs at Princeton University, claims that many undocumented immigrants from Mexico return to their homeland after performing seasonal labor in the United States. Massey argues that building a border wall would only trap Mexican migrants in the United States.

A plan for more walls to further enhance border enforcement is moronic not only because it is expensive. Abundant evidence also shows that money spent on border enforcement is worse than useless— it's counterproductive. For most of the 20th century, migration from Mexico was heavily circular, with male migrants moving back and forth across the border to earn money in the United States and then returning to Mexico to spend and invest at home. . . .

Although the intent of border enforcement was to discourage migrants from coming to the United States, in practice it backfired, instead discouraging them from returning home to Mexico. Having experienced the risks and having paid the costs of gaining entry, undocumented men increasingly hunkered down and stayed in the United States, rather than circulating back to face the gantlet once more.

Douglas Massey, "Donald Trump's Mexican Border Wall Is a Moronic Idea," *Foreign Policy*, August 18, 2015. www.foreignpolicy.com.

**VIEWPOINT**

for people is going to provide prosperity to the United States, he is completely crazy."[49]

# Environmental Impact of a Border Wall

The idea of sealing off the southern US border has also come under fire for reasons that have nothing to do with money. Environmentalists claim a wall would be detrimental to wildlife and ecosystems in the border region. According to journalist and filmmaker Boonsri Dickinson, "Most of the [current] wall was built without any regard to environmental laws. In 2005, Congress gave the Department of Homeland Security the authority to waive all laws in order to hasten construction." According to Dickinson, concerned environmentalists have noted that the barriers that are already in place along parts of the border interrupt migration and watering hole pathways of bison, wolves, jaguars, and bighorn sheep. As Dickinson writes, "Humans can find gaps in the wall. But the animals can't."[50]

> "Most of the [current] wall was built without any regard to environmental laws. In 2005, Congress gave the Department of Homeland Security the authority to waive all laws in order to hasten construction."[50]
>
> —Boonsri Dickinson, journalist and filmmaker.

Experts warn that such impediments to the free movement of some animals can threaten their survival. A few animals in some of the larger wildlife refuges in the region are already endangered. A 2011 University of Texas study found that habitat ranges had been reduced for threatened species of turtles, frogs, toads, and even small cats such as the jaguarondi and ocelot because of the current walls. Some small "doorways" have been left in parts of the fence to allow small animals to pass through, but Jesse Lasky, a biology professor at Penn State and coauthor of the Texas study, says, "These sorts of projects are only Band-Aids. The cure is to leave key wildlife areas barrier-free."[51]

Normally, government infrastructure projects of this magnitude cannot proceed without environmental impact studies, but the DHS was able to skirt this requirement via the REAL ID Act of 2005. This piece of legislation came in the wake of the 2001 terrorist attacks on America. In part it gave the government the power to forgo such studies if the intended project fell under the protective banner of national security. The border wall was deemed a national security issue. In 2009 the DHS signed an agreement with the US Department of the Interior to set aside $50 million in funds to carry out environmental studies and mitigate habitat damage done by wall-building projects. According to the *Arizona Republic*, $6.8 million of that sum was spent the following year on impact studies, but "customs officials couldn't immediately identify further spending on border mitigation efforts."[52] Therefore, no further studies were carried out.

## A Virtual Wall, a Solid Barrier, or Both?

In part to reduce costs and environmental impact, the George W. Bush administration authorized SBInet in 2006. This project aimed at beefing up electronic detection methods—including ground-level sensors, infrared radar towers, and aerial drones—instead of investing in physical barriers. The sensors activate cameras to capture movements through protected areas and alert border patrol agents to possible illegal entries. The DHS spent $1 billion on SBInet sensors to cover 53 miles (85 km) of the Arizona-Mexico border. However, "Only 1% of the alarm calls they created led to arrests,"[53] the BBC News reported in an August 2012 article. The system was scheduled to be operational in 2011, but technology issues and costs led to a halt to expansion in that year.

In 2014 the Obama administration approved the deployment of sensor towers along the same border in an effort to revive the virtual fence solution. The CBP estimates that it will take ten years and cost between $500 million and $700 million to cover that stretch of the border. An Israeli firm—expert in using such technology along its country's border—has already undertaken the contract. Whether the new construction will progress further than SBInet, no one can say. However, the commitment to a nonphysical barrier suggests that the government has options other than walling off the United States from Mexico.

Some politicians and commentators believe that a physical wall or fence is the only sure deterrent to illegal immigration. Chris Simcox, the cofounder and former spokesperson for the Minuteman

In 2007, at a Border Patrol processing center in El Paso, Texas, members of the Texas National Guard monitor dozens of cameras for illegal border crossings. Electronic sensors, authorized the previous year, activate cameras that capture movements along the border.

Civil Defense Corps, a freelance group of border watchers, says, "The 'virtual' fence is a diplomacy ploy; it is about appeasing foreign and domestic special interests. The feds need to get serious about national security, and put some of their taxpayer-paid time, effort and funding into building [a] fence, not fairy tales."[54]

Others, however, contend that building a contiguous wall is not going to stop illegals. Those who want to get in, they argue, will find a way. Democratic representative Henry Cuellar of Texas's 28th district (a region that shares a large part of the border with Mexico) compares US efforts at fence building to the attempts of the Chinese Ming dynasty to keep out the Mongol hordes by erecting the Great Wall of China. "Simply stated, a fence is a 14th century solution to a 21st century problem,"[55] Cuellar said in a 2013 Forbes interview. He notes that many undocumented immigrants cross the border legally on work visas but never go home; others are smuggled in. So he believes a wall is of limited use.

US Border Patrol officer Robert Duff insists that the physical barrier is simply part of an overall effort to combat illegal immigration. "Fencing is not the end all, be all," Duff remarks in a National Public Radio report. "I started my career in San Diego and saw them construct the initial fence, and then two and three layers of fencing. They'll go over it, they'll go under it, they'll go through it. A fence does not seal the border. It helps, but it's not the solution."[56] The solution, though, remains the subject of debate. As ongoing calls to build a permanent barrier between the United States and Mexico demonstrate, some Americans believe such extreme measures are necessary to keep the nation secure and stem the tide of illegal immigrants. Others contend that a wall would not be practical or effective. What's more, it sends the message that America is no longer—as the poem engraved on the Statue of Liberty promises—a haven for the world's "huddled masses yearning to breathe free" but a fortress willing to open its gates for some but not all.

> "Simply stated, a fence is a 14th century solution to a 21st century problem."[55]
>
> —Henry Cuellar, Democratic US representative from Texas.

# Should Illegal Immigrants Be Deported?

In January 2016 the DHS began a nationwide sweep to deport the more than one hundred thousand illegal immigrants that had fled escalating violence and poverty in Guatemala, El Salvador, and Honduras in 2013 and 2014. These Central Americans crossed the Mexican border often in fear for their lives. "If these families are deported—and most of them would be women and children, they would be returned to places they fled to escape being killed, raped or tortured,"[57] says Kica Matos, a spokesperson for the Fair Immigration Reform Movement. Some sought refuge in American courts, where their asylum appeals are still pending; others faded into communities across the land in hopes of not being found. But ICE began raiding homes in Georgia and Texas to make clear its commitment. "Our border is not open to illegal immigration, and if individuals come here illegally, do not qualify for asylum or other relief, and have final orders of removal, they will be sent back consistent with our laws and our values,"[58] said Gillian Christensen, an ICE spokesperson.

## Obama's Policy on Deportations

The US government has ramped up its deportations of illegals in recent years. The Obama administration deported close to 2 million unauthorized immigrants over the first five years of his presidency. During the last year of the George W. Bush administration, the DHS reported that more than 359,000 illegals had been removed from the country by court order. Removals do not include the number of illegals caught and returned at the border. In the year Obama took office in 2009, the number of removals climbed to 391,597, and by 2013 (the last year the DHS has on record), the number was 438,421. Removals are usually carried out by ICE agents, and in 59 percent of the cases on record, the individuals earmarked for removal had been convicted of a crime. The number of removals has prompted some immigrants' rights advocates to call Obama the "deporter in chief" because his numbers exceed those of previous presidents.

In February 2014, however, Obama enacted an executive order to modify specific immigration legislation to help shield families from deportation. He mandated changes to the 2012 Deferred Action for Childhood Arrivals (DACA) policy. DACA exempted illegal immigrants who were under thirty-one years of age (and claimed to have entered the country before their sixteenth birthday) from deportation. It also allowed them to apply for a work

After illegally entering Texas from Mexico with her family in 2014, an eight-year-old girl from El Salvador awaits processing. Thousands of families fled escalating violence and poverty in their Central American homelands in 2013 and 2014.

permit that could be renewed every two years. The 2014 mandates expanded coverage to those who entered the country as a child before 2010 regardless of current age and increased the work permit renewal period to three years. Also in 2014, Obama announced another executive action—the Deferred Action for Parents of Americans and Lawful Permanent Residents (DAPA)—to delay deportation of parents of children covered by DACA. According to the White House, the two programs would protect about 5 million undocumented immigrants from deportation.

In December 2014 Texas and twenty-five other states sued the US government over implementation of DAPA and the DACA expansions. A Texas judge blocked these programs from going into effect, and a federal appeals court agreed that Obama had exceeded his authority. A legal brief from the Cato Institute in support of the lawsuit highlighted the basic argument: "While we agree that the immigration laws need to be overhauled and sympathize with the plight facing undocumented immigrants, the path designed by the Framers for implementing needed reforms goes through the halls of Congress. Unilateral exercises of power such as DAPA undermine the separation of powers and ultimately the rule of law."[59] The case reached the US Supreme Court in 2016. A 4-4 tie vote by the justices in June 2016 left in place a lower court ruling that the president had exceeded his powers when he altered immigration laws by executive order. The ruling does not mean that millions more will now be deported, but it does raise questions about the validity of actions taken under the two programs.

## US Workers Suffer

Critics of Obama's executive actions on immigration contend that it is Congress's role to enact immigration policy, not the president's. The legislature sets limits on immigration in part to maintain good wages for US citizens by ensuring that unlawful immigrants do not flood the job market. Congress permits some immigrants to work in the country through a visa program. However, work visas are temporary, and visitors who have them (approximately 140,000 are granted each year) are supposed to leave the country when their visas expire. Opponents to DACA and DAPA claim that the president's actions have upset these checks and balances by supplying hundreds of thousands—and potentially millions—of undocumented workers with work permits. "Once given work authorization, illegal immigrants are more likely to compete with Americans for better-paying jobs," says Steven A. Camarota of the Center for Immigration Studies. Less-educated US citizens often try to improve their futures by seeking out better-paying unskilled jobs—such as security guards, janitors, and clerks—that also provide insurance and other benefits. "These relatively well-paying jobs for the non-college educated will now open up to illegal immigrants," Camarota warns. "That may well benefit illegal immigrants, but may also reduce the job prospects of natives."[60]

> "Unilateral exercises of power such as DAPA undermine the separation of powers and ultimately the rule of law."[59]
>
> —The Cato Institute, a libertarian research organization.

Many Americans believe that current laws and presidential decrees should not leave the country so vulnerable to waves of more illegal immigration. All Republican candidates seeking the presidential nomination in 2016 had vowed to repeal DACA and DAPA if elected, and Republican lawmakers had introduced bills to repeal these acts. In August 2014, for instance, Republicans in the House of Representatives passed a bill that would strip the delayed deportation status of those young enough to be covered by DACA. Though the bill did not pass Congress, it indicates a staunch belief that the threat of deportation, coupled with obstacles to lawful work status, is what keeps illegals from overwhelming the nation and its native or otherwise documented workforce. "Immigrants need to follow proper procedures to enter this country or they should be deported,"[61] attests one letter writer to the *Buffalo News* in 2014. The letter writer's point is that the law already provides immigrants with a means to achieve the privileges of legal residency, and those who violate that law should be sent back. Indeed, according to a July 2014 Rasmussen Reports poll after the crossing of tens of thousands of unaccompanied children fleeing violence in Central America, 59 percent of US voters said they "believe the primary focus of any new immigration legislation passed by Congress should be to send the young illegal immigrants back home as quickly as possible." Only 27 percent said the government should make it "easier for these illegal immigrants to remain in the United States."[62] An April 2015 Rasmussen Reports poll found that 62 percent of voters believe the government is not aggressive enough in deporting illegal immigrants, while 51 percent disagreed with the president's plan to exempt parents of legalized children from deportation.

## No Place for Deportees to Go

A large percentage of Americans, however, believe that deportation is not the best solution to America's immigration problems. Many agree that illegal immigrants who have committed serious crimes should be removed from the nation but that the majority of illegals are peaceful individuals or families who have simply come to the United States to seek opportunities. Martine Kalaw, a refugee from Zambia whose parents died before securing her legal status, argues that often illegals have no place to return to because of tragic circumstances in their home countries. Kalaw's parents, for example, were natives of the Democratic Republic of Congo, a war-torn nation in which civilians suffer poverty, malnutrition, and other traumas associated with ongoing conflicts.

"Immigrants need to follow proper procedures to enter this country or they should be deported."[61]

—Tom Camizzi, a New York resident.

In a 2016 *Huffington Post* blog article, Kalaw says that when she was threatened with deportation, she believed "the U.S. government was getting rid of me to teach my deceased parents a lesson for failing to secure my status." According to Kalaw, Zambia had rejected her return, and she feared for her life when an immigration judge offered to send her back to her parents' homeland. She had actually lived in the United States for seventeen years and had, as an orphan, pursued an education without public assistance. "He thought I should be sent to the Democratic Republic of Congo despite its human rights violations such as systematic rape of women specifically in Eastern Congo and war taking place there," Kalaw explains. "Our impulse is to want to send illegal immigrants back to where they belong, but it's imperative for us to

Women displaced by ethnic violence in the Democratic Republic of Congo carry bags of coal to a refugee camp. The threat of deportation can be terrifying to someone who fled a country that is plagued by extreme violence and poverty.

be well-informed before making such decisions. Let's first consider the circumstances in which they ended up in our nation," Kalaw reminds her readers. "We ought to also recognize the possibility that some of them may in fact belong in the U.S."[63]

While Kalaw's case may be unusual compared to the streams of Mexican immigrants crossing the border, the experiences of deported Mexicans bear some resemblances. In a November 2014 *National Geographic* article, Mexican officials in Tijuana spoke of the thousands of illegals who are returned to this well-known border town each year. Gilberto Martinez, administrator of Casa del Migrante, a nonprofit organization, says that most of these immigrants leave the country full of hope for a new life. Once caught on the other side, however, he says they are returned "sad, exhausted, beaten, as if they're coming from a funeral."[64] Sam Quinones, the

# President Obama's Deportation Efforts Are Very Lax

Political columnist Red Jahncke claims that Barack Obama has been very soft on illegal immigrants. He insists that too many of those caught by ICE are simply let go instead of being deported.

By law, illegal immigrants who have received a "final removal order" are to be deported. President Obama is not doing so. Indeed, he claims authority to exempt millions from enforcement.

As a result, the number of illegal residents who have been apprehended but not detained or deported has swelled to nearly 2 million, as reflected on the "non-detained docket," an almost secret list maintained by Immigration and Customs Enforcement. About half of those on the ICE docket have received a final removal order from an immigration court judge. . . .

The extent of Obama's non-enforcement is startling. In 2015, ICE carried out only 235,000 "removals," including 135,000 convicted criminals (that's enforcement of criminal law) and 90,000 non-Mexicans captured by Border Patrol and turned over to ICE for removal. (That's interdiction, not deportation.) That leaves only 10,000 deported for violation of our immigration laws.

Red Jahncke, "Restart Deportation as a Way of Deterring Illegal Immigrants," *Investor's Business Daily*, February 4, 2016. www.investors.com.

author of the article, describes the difficult fate of these deportees. "These men—90 percent of the deportees are men—live in a kind of limbo. Most have been in America so long that they have lost ties to Mexico. They remain in Tijuana to be close to their families in the United States, to try to cross again, or because they no longer know anyone in their Mexican hometowns,"[65] says Quinones. He adds that many of these 1.3 million rootless inhabitants of Tijuana cannot find work in Mexico because they lack any papers that identify them as citizens of that country.

# The Costs of Deportation

Deportation does break up families. On the Families for Freedom website, Julio Beltre recounted how his father was taken away in shackles and returned to the Dominican Republic, leaving Julio and two siblings behind. Families for Freedom is an advocacy group sponsoring legislation that would allow children to testify

## President Obama's Deportation Efforts Are Very Stringent

**VIEWPOINT**

Alejandra Marchevsky is a professor of liberal studies and gender studies at California State University–Los Angeles, and her colleague, Beth Baker, is a professor of anthropology there. Together, these two maintain that Barack Obama has aggressively deported a large number of undocumented immigrants as criminals even though many of these individuals have only committed minor offenses.

> Since taking the oath of office, Obama has deported immigrants at a faster rate than any other president in US history, nearly a record 2 million people. On a typical day, there are over 30,000 immigrants imprisoned in the world's largest immigration detention system. Most deportees never see an attorney or have a hearing before a judge before they are expelled from the country. . . .
>
> Immigration and Customs Enforcement (ICE) recently reported that 59 percent of deportations in fiscal year 2013 involved noncitizens with criminal records. Yet, what ICE did not highlight is that the vast majority of criminal deportees were expelled for non-violent offenses, with 60 percent convicted of misdemeanors punishable by less than one year in prison. In 2012, less than one percent of such deportations involved homicide convictions.

Alejandra Marchevsky and Beth Baker, "Why Has President Obama Deported More Immigrants than Any President in US History?," *Nation*, March 31, 2014. www.nation.com.

for their parents at deportation hearings. On a fact sheet for the proposed bill is the plea of six-year-old Alejandra Barrios: "I love my father. I'm very sad they came and took my papi away in hand-cuffs and deported him to Mexico. My papi never got a parking ticket, he never gets drunk, he works everyday. I want to tell the judge how good he is, but they won't let me."[66] Captured illegals who are parents of children born in the United States are given a difficult choice. They can have their children deported to their homelands to face the same problems the family was fleeing or leave them with relatives or foster agencies in the United States.

In an August 2012 report, the Center for American Progress estimated that foster care costs the government about $26,000 per child of deportee parents. Foster care is only one of the costs associated with deportation, however. The American Action Forum, a research think tank, points out that deporting every illegal immigrant would involve apprehension, detainment, and transport

Demonstrators protest deportations that split up families. Children who were born in the United States, and are thus citizens, are sometimes separated from their parents, who entered the country illegally, were caught, and were deported.

back to home countries. In a March 2015 assessment, the organization claimed this would involve hiring tens of thousands of new ICE agents as well as bolstering holding facilities and hiring legal staff. The resulting tax-dollar costs would fall between $419 billion and $620 billion. "Not only would enforcing current law cost taxpayers, it would also burden the economy," say Ben Gitis and Laura Collins of the American Action Forum. These authors insist that mass deportations would reduce the nation's earning power. "Removing all undocumented immigrants would cause the labor force to shrink by 6.4 percent, which translates to a loss of 11 million workers," Gitis and Collins explain. "As a result, 20 years from now the economy would be nearly 6 percent or $1.6 trillion smaller than it would be if the government did not remove all undocumented immigrants."[67]

> "Removing all undocumented immigrants would cause the labor force to shrink by 6.4 percent, which translates to a loss of 11 million workers."[67]
>
> —Ben Gitis and Laura Collins, members of the American Action Forum.

## The Costs of Allowing Illegal Immigrants to Stay

Some believe these figures are too high. When told of the American Action Forum's predicted deportation price tag, Republican presidential candidate Donald Trump said that the numbers were simply wrong and that better management would reduce costs. Others contend that the cost of removal still pales in comparison to the costs America bears for allowing illegals to stay or granting amnesty to this population.

For example, in 2013 the Heritage Foundation, a conservative think tank, studied the cost of government assistance programs that families consumed in America. According to Robert Rector and Jason Richwine, the authors of this study, typical families pay for and use benefits such as Medicare, unemployment insurance, and workers' compensation, as well as services that include police, fire, and highways. Low-income families also consume more than $900 billion in assistance programs such as food stamps, Medicaid, and public housing, Rector and Richwine assert. While better-off families with college-educated heads of household use fewer of these benefits and thus tend to pay more in taxes than they consume in aid, poorer families with undereducated heads of household typically consume more aid than they pay in taxes. The authors insist, "The high deficits of poorly educated households are important in the amnesty debate because the typical unlawful immigrant has only a 10th-grade education. Half of unlawful immigrant households are headed by an individual with less than a high school degree, and another 25 percent of household heads have only a high school degree."[68]

> "Over a lifetime, the former unlawful immigrants together would receive $9.4 trillion in government benefits and services and pay $3.1 trillion in taxes. They would generate a lifetime fiscal deficit (total benefits minus total taxes) of $6.3 trillion."[69]
>
> —Robert Rector and Jason Richwine, members of the Heritage Foundation.

Rector and Richwine acknowledge that undocumented adults often cannot take advantage of many government assistance benefits because of their illegal status, but any of their children born in the country can. If amnesty is granted, then the low-skilled, poorly educated adult population will be suddenly given these benefits as well, increasing the costs over time as adults move from workers to retirees. According to Rector and Richwine, "Over a lifetime, the former unlawful immigrants together would receive $9.4 trillion in government benefits and services and pay $3.1 trillion in taxes. They would generate a lifetime fiscal deficit (total benefits minus total taxes) of $6.3 trillion."[69] This total, the authors argue, would—as always—be borne by the taxpayers.

## The Consequences of Contradictory Policies

Despite Obama's attempts to grant more protections to some undocumented individuals, ICE roundups under his watch were conducted more vigorously in the early part of 2016. The seemingly contradictory policies have confused both the president's supporters and opponents. Some observers blame the recent rise in border crossers from Central America partly on the lack of clarity concerning the country's approach to immigration. That is, many of these immigrants might think that America is now welcoming illegals or at least not turning them away once they are safely across the border. The hope of amnesty and the fact that so many cases involving deportation are being disputed in the courts may signal that this is an opportune time to take the risk.

However, the editorial staff of Bloomberg View claims that "with the future of U.S. immigration policy clouded by political uncertainty and legal challenges, both the emigrants and those who seek to exploit them need a clarifying reminder that the U.S. will enforce its immigration laws."[70] They see the stepped-up ICE raids as an assertion that America will not be a nation of open borders. Instead, the government and its agents must still respect the law, however much its policies are in debate and subject to reform.

# Should the United States Employ a Path to Citizenship for Illegal Immigrants?

CHAPTER

In 2007 and 2008 Barack Obama made several campaign promises regarding immigration reform during his bid for presidency. His platform stressed the importance of secure borders to curb the numbers of illegals entering the country, but for those already in the United States, Obama pushed for greater tolerance. According to him, the millions of undocumented workers and their families had labored for the good of the country and yet could not appreciate the benefits of citizenship. In fact, they had to live in hiding, fearful of losing jobs or being deported. Obama wanted to bring these people "out of the shadows" to join in the great immigrant heritage of the United States. His immigration agenda called on the nation to "support a system that allows undocumented immigrants who are in good standing to pay a fine, learn English, and go to the back of the line for the opportunity to become citizens."[71] Borrowing a phrase that had been around for many years, Obama and his backers dubbed this plan a "pathway to citizenship." It was designed to reward those who wanted to do the right thing. His detractors termed it "amnesty," the setting of a dangerous precedent for those who had broken the law.

## Avoiding the A-Word

Although many of his critics argue that Obama's ongoing effort to forgive undocumented workers for having entered the country illegally is a political and practical misstep, he was not the first executive to support amnesty. Ronald Reagan, a conservative icon, signed an immigration reform bill in 1986 that granted 3 million undocumented workers who had entered the country before 1982 "legalized" status. The goal was to stop what many saw as an exploitive relationship between American business owners and the low-paid immigrants who worked for them. By avoiding the "politically toxic A-word," Reagan was able to effect change, his political compatriots acknowledge in a National Public Radio retrospective. "We used the word 'legalization,'" former Wyoming senator Alan K. Simpson said in the broadcast. "And everybody fell asleep lightly for a while, and we were able to do legalization."[72] Even though legalization was, for practical purposes, the same as amnesty, many politicians shied away from the latter word. It suggested a disregard for US laws and an invitation to others to cross America's borders with impunity. Still, Simpson, a Republican, maintains that Reagan believed he was doing the right thing by helping people who otherwise had no rights.

Obama, facing a Republican-led Congress, has also kept his distance from the term *amnesty*. Even so, he has insisted throughout much of his tenure as president that he would not sign a new immigration reform bill that did not include a pathway to citizenship for the millions of illegals already in the country. In July 2013 he told a Spanish television news station in Denver, "It

*President Barack Obama has long supported a path to citizenship for undocumented immigrants. Even before he was elected president, he promoted both tolerance and secure borders.*

does not make sense to me, if we're going to make this once-in-a-generation effort to finally fix the system, to leave the status of 11 million people or so unresolved." By not affording a pathway to those who already resided in the United States, Obama claimed the nation was revealing an ugly contentedness to keep illegal immigrants "permanently resigned to a lower status. That's not who we are as Americans." In a later appearance on a Dallas station, he remarked, "It's time for us to stop worrying about politics and worry about doing the right thing for the country."[73]

## Following the Path to Citizenship

Commonly, immigrants who come to the United States can become naturalized citizens by first acquiring a Permanent Resident Card (green card), which lets them live and work in the country. After holding a green card for five years (fewer years for spouses of US residents and military personnel), immigrants can apply to become citizens. To begin the process, they must prove that they are at least eighteen years of age, and they must file required

*Legal immigrants can become naturalized US citizens by first acquiring a Permanent Resident Card—better known as a green card (even though the cards have been different colors over the years). This card enables immigrants to live and work in the United States.*

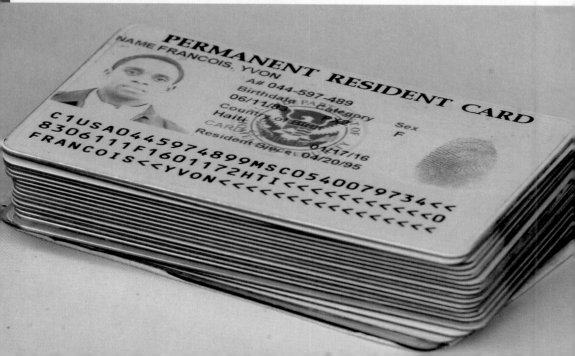

papers and pay a fee. The application process can take from six months to a year to complete. At the end, prospective citizens must take an exam to demonstrate that they are able to read, write, and speak English; are of good moral character; and accept the laws of the Constitution. Children born on US soil are not required to follow the process to become citizens. They are granted birthright citizenship even if their parents are not lawful citizens.

In 2013 the White House's plan for immigration reform mandated a path to citizenship for the 11 million undocumented immigrants who had not followed the legal procedures to attain permanent residency. Obama has largely stood by that measure. According to his administration's requirements, "Undocumented immigrants must come forward and register, submit biometric data, pass criminal background and national security checks, and pay fees and penalties before they will be eligible for a provisional legal status."[74] These people then must wait their turn behind all other legal applicants seeking green cards and then submit to the process of becoming a citizen. The president maintains that all who are given "provisional" status will not be able to partake of certain welfare or tax benefits until they finish their journey and become full citizens.

> "It does not make sense to me, if we're going to make this once-in-a-generation effort to finally fix the system, to leave the status of 11 million people or so unresolved."[73]
>
> —Barack Obama, forty-fourth president of the United States.

These stipulations went into a vast immigration reform bill in 2013. It was a piece of legislation initiated by and passed in the Senate with endorsement by key Republican and Democratic congressional leaders. The bill, however, was not taken up in the House of Representatives, due to resistance from Republicans there. In July 2013 House Speaker John Boehner (a Republican from Ohio) responded to critics by stating, "I've made it clear and I'll make it clear again, the House does not intend to take up the Senate bill. The House is going to do its own job in developing an immigration bill."[75] Such a bill was drafted, but it focused more on border security than attempts to deal with the illegal population. The pathway to citizenship—or even legalization—provisions have appeared in other bills, but none have gained traction in the House of Representatives.

## The Advantages of a Path to Citizenship

According to those who support a pathway to citizenship, the advantages of such a policy outweigh any disadvantages. A couple of years before the start of the Obama presidency, Jared Bernstein, a member of the Economic Policy Institute, argued that a path to citizenship would help reduce the poverty rate among illegals. "There is a huge difference between the economic status of immigrants who have become citizens and those who have not," Bernstein wrote in 2006. "The path to citizenship is also a path out of poverty."[76]

> "Legal status would boost the economy, but the resulting productivity and wage gains would be much higher if the vast majority of the undocumented population are granted citizenship."[77]
>
> —Esther Yu-Hsi Lee, immigration reporter for Think Progress.

Others speak of national economic gains through job creation and taxes. For example, Esther Yu-Hsi Lee, a contributor to the Think Progress website, claims that citizenship would be better than continuing efforts by Republicans to grant legal status to undocumented immigrants. "Legal status would boost the economy, but the resulting productivity and wage gains would be much higher if the vast majority of the undocumented population are granted citizenship," Lee writes in a 2014 article. According to Lee, the gains would be markedly different:

> Researchers found that immigrants who are only eligible for legal status, but not citizenship, would contribute about $832 billion to the economy in a ten year period, add 121,000 more jobs per year, and pay $109 billion in taxes over a ten year period. Compare that to a scenario where undocumented immigrants are granted legal status and citizenship at the same time, the U.S. GDP [gross domestic product] would grow by $1.4 trillion over a ten year period, immigrants would help to create an additional 203,000 jobs per year, and add $184 billion in tax revenue.[77]

Lee's numbers come from a 2013 White House report in which Cecilia Muñoz and Gene Sperling contend that citizenship has fiscal benefits for immigrants beyond wage gain and the ability to travel for work. "The largest factor, however, may be the less tangible one: greater certainty that accompanies citizenship leads to more investment, for example, in education and training, or more willingness to take the risk of starting a business,"[78] the authors maintain.

## The Pitfalls of a Pathway to Citizenship

Opponents of the pathway to citizenship claim that the national fiscal burden will be greater than the economic rewards. Most focus on the increased welfare resources that former illegals will be able to tap. Republicans on the Senate Budget Committee, for example, estimate that once the provisional status period ends, these costs "could be upwards of $40 billion in 2022 alone, just for Medicaid and Obamacare."[79] Medicaid is a joint health care program funded by the states and the federal government. It assists low-income individuals and families. Obamacare is a nickname given to the Affordable Care Act, a law passed in 2010 that increases access to health care and health insurance for Americans who do not have work-sponsored insurance. Public health care systems like Medicaid and Obamacare are funded through tax money. The taxes an individual contributes to these programs are expected to cover that individual's use of medical services in the future. However, in reality, the money collected today simply gets paid out to poorer families and older people who draw on those services now.

Thus, there is an unfunded gap between what the programs take in today and what they promise to pay in the future. This problem, critics say, will get worse if the nation adds a huge number of illegal immigrants to the roles of eligible users. Members of the Senate Budget Committee worry that once provisional status for undocumented workers ends, that unfunded gap would increase by another $2 trillion in the long term. These senators go on to claim, "The net costs would be enormous and only increase once citizenship is granted (and would extend to our nation's retirement programs as well)."[80] Promoting these figures, Fox News

# Legalizing the Current Undocumented Population Will Harm the US Economy

Jim DeMint and Robert Rector of the Heritage Foundation, a conservative think tank, argue that America cannot support both open borders and a robust welfare system. In their view, the cost of government services to illegal immigrants will cripple the US economy.

In addition to being unfair to those who follow the law and encouraging more unlawful immigration in the future, amnesty has a substantial price tag.

An exhaustive study by the Heritage Foundation has found that after amnesty, current unlawful immigrants would receive $9.4 trillion in government benefits and services and pay more than $3 trillion in taxes over their lifetimes. That leaves a net fiscal deficit (benefits minus taxes) of $6.3 trillion. That deficit would have to be financed by increasing the government debt or raising taxes on U.S. citizens.

For centuries immigration has been vital to our nation's health, and it will be essential to our future success. Yet immigrants should come to our nation lawfully and should not impose additional fiscal costs on our overburdened taxpayers.

Jim DeMint and Robert Rector, "Amnesty for Illegal Immigrants Will Cost America," *Washington Post*, May 6, 2013. www.washingtonpost.com.

adds, "Payments from Medicaid and subsidies from the federal health care law represent just a fraction of federal government benefits that a green-card holder or U.S. citizen can apply for."[81]

Other experts are concerned that a pathway to citizenship would be a logistical nightmare and may not resolve some nagging nonfinancial immigration issues. Peter Skerry, a political science professor and a senior fellow at the Brookings Institution, insists that putting millions of illegals in line with legal immigrants awaiting citizenship will simply bog down the process. He notes that some legal immigrants have been waiting twenty years for green cards, so consigning illegals to the back of the line is not a promise to afford the rights of citizenship any time soon. Skerry also claims that many illegals are unsure of where their loyalty lies and that some come to work in the United States fully expecting to return to their native countries with the profits of their labor. "Of the 2.7 million who qualified for the amnesty granted

## Legalizing the Current Undocumented Population Will Help the US Economy

Raúl Hinojosa-Ojeda, director of the North American Integration and Development Center, argues that comprehensive immigration reform that legalizes current undocumented immigrants will greatly benefit America's economy.

Comprehensive immigration reform would increase U.S. GDP by at least 0.84 percent per year. Using 10-year GDP projections prepared by the Congressional Budget Office, this translates into a steadily increasing amount of added annual GDP over the coming decade. The 10-year total is at least $1.5 trillion in added GDP, which includes roughly $1.2 trillion in additional consumption and $256 billion in additional investment.

Comprehensive immigration reform brings substantial economic gains even in the short run—during the first three years following legalization. The real wages of newly legalized workers increase by roughly $4,400 per year among those in less-skilled jobs during the first three years of implementation, and $6,185 per year for those in higher-skilled jobs. The higher earning power of newly legalized workers translates into an increase in net personal income of $30 billion to $36 billion, which would generate $4.5 to $5.4 billion in additional net tax revenue nationally, enough to support 750,000 to 900,000 new jobs.

Raúl Hinojosa-Ojeda, "The Economic Benefits of Comprehensive Immigration Reform," *Cato Journal*, Winter 2012, p. 189.

**VIEWPOINT**

by Congress in 1986, barely 41 percent had become citizens as of 2009," Skerry writes of legalization during the Reagan years. "After nearly a quarter century, the rest have remained permanent residents with green cards. Simply put, not all illegal immigrants are sure they want to be US citizens."[82] Permanent residents can be legally employed and can access welfare, but they do not have the right to vote in US elections and have restrictions on travel outside of the country. Granting illegals permanent noncitizen resident status would be a better option, Skerry says. It would impose a penalty on those who flouted US laws but still give them a means to legitimately work and raise their families in their adopted land.

> "Not all illegal immigrants are sure they want to be US citizens."[82]
>
> —Peter Skerry, senior fellow at the Brookings Institution and a political science professor at Boston College.

## Public Views on Creating a Pathway

Despite warnings against costs and other potential problems, most Americans favor the creation of a pathway to citizenship for the nation's illegal immigrant population. An August 2015 Gallup Poll found that 65 percent of Americans believe undocumented immigrants should be allowed to remain in the country and work toward citizenship over time. Only 14 percent maintain that illegals should only be allowed to work for a limited time, and 19 percent advocate deportation. Similarly, a March 2016 Public Religion Research Institute poll of more than forty-two thousand Americans reported that 19 percent endorse deportation, while 62 percent would allow illegals to stay and earn citizenship by meeting certain requirements. Fifteen percent favor a plan that would allow them to remain but not become citizens.

Demographic trends in these polls reveal much about those who favor a pathway to citizenship. For instance, the Gallup Poll showed that 77 percent of Hispanics and 70 percent of African Americans support a pathway policy. The results also indicated that non-Hispanic whites (20 percent) were more likely to favor deportation than either blacks (14 percent) or Hispanics (8 percent). The Public Religion poll noted that the age of those surveyed also corresponded to specific responses. Roughly 69 percent of young people (ages eighteen to twenty-nine) back a pathway to citizenship, whereas only 11 percent agree with deportation. Of those older Americans (age sixty-five and over), only 58 percent endorse the creation of a pathway, while 23 percent favor deportation.

A February 2016 Rasmussen Reports poll of one thousand likely voters discovered that even if the majority support giving a pathway to illegals, 59 percent believe that gaining control of the border should be immigration reform's top priority, while only 34 percent think that granting citizenship to the undocumented population in the country is a more pressing issue. In fact, the poll found that 52 percent of Americans believed that initiating a pathway to citizenship will simply invite more illegal immigration. Jeb Bush, the former governor of Florida and former candidate for the Republican presidential nomination in 2016, made that argument in a book he coauthored in 2013. "It is absolutely vital to the integrity of our immigration system that actions have consequences," he and Clint Bolick state in *Immigration Wars: Forging an American Solution*. "A grant of citizenship is an undeserving reward for conduct that we cannot afford to encourage."[83]

## The Future of Pathway Policy Making

In a 2014 CNN interview, Obama seemed to suggest that he would forgo a pathway to citizenship in an immigration bill if it meant that Congress would move forward on some collective reform legislation. In January of that year, reporter Nick Chiles of the Atlanta Black Star stated, "Clearly the president has decided that a new bill that allows undocumented immigrants to gain some legal status is better than nothing."[84] According to Chiles, the president responded favorably to a Republican plan that offered illegal immigrants legalized status as opposed to citizenship. The president hoped such a plan would allow that population a chance to become citizens through normal naturalization processes once they were "legalized." In the CNN interview, the president explained the need for compromise: "The question is, is there more that we can do in this legislation that gets both Democratic and

*Young immigrants from many different countries take the oath of allegiance during a citizenship ceremony in Chicago, Illinois. Like President Obama, Hillary Clinton has stated her support for a path to citizenship for undocumented immigrants.*

Republican support but solves these broader problems, including strengthening borders and making sure that we have a legal immigration system that works better than it currently does."[85]

To some observers, the president's comments hinted that his position on the issue was softening. However, no such compromise has gone into effect, because Congress has not collectively come forward with a reform plan. Obama's Democratic ally, Hillary Clinton, the front-runner for the Democratic presidential ticket in 2016, said she supported Obama's efforts (including his executive actions related to illegal immigration) and vowed to make a path to citizenship the centerpiece of her immigration reform policy. At a campaign event in Las Vegas, Nevada, Clinton told a crowd that included undocumented immigrants that she was against "legalization" offered by Republican lawmakers. "When they talk about 'legal status,' that is code for 'second-class status,'"[86] Clinton stated.

The pathway to citizenship strategy has served as a major talking point in immigration reform debates for more than a decade. What both Obama and Clinton's rhetoric reveals, though, is that promises and proclamations do not easily translate into law. Some observers, like Vivek Wadhwa, an academic and technology entrepreneur, argue that the focus on citizenship—and its divisiveness among lawmakers—keeps derailing the larger issue of immigration reform. "We keep talking about citizenship as if it's the ultimate thing," Wadhwa states. "We should just get this immigration reform done and come back 10 years from now and solve the issue of citizenship."[87] However, many do not see the advantage of delaying a resolution. Advocates of a pathway to citizenship claim that illegals should not be made to wait another decade to fully take part in the country they call home. At the same time, opponents of this proposed policy insist the nation cannot tolerate another ten years of mass illegal immigration brought on by continually dangling the carrot of possible citizenship. Reconciling these two viewpoints into a coherent immigration plan has remained a challenge for lawmakers. Accepting any form of immigration reform that favors one view over the other has proved difficult for the nation as a whole.

"It is absolutely vital to the integrity of our immigration system that actions have consequences. A grant of citizenship is an undeserving reward for conduct that we cannot afford to encourage."[83]

—Jeb Bush, former governor of Florida and a former Republican candidate for president, and author Clint Bolick.

## Introduction: "The Price of the American Dream"

1. Quoted in Bigad Shaban, "'You Have to Live in Fear': One Undocumented Immigrant's Story," *CBS News*, November 22, 2014. www.cbsnews.com.
2. Quoted in Shaban, "'You Have to Live in Fear.'"
3. Xavier Becerra, "Immigrants Deserve a Path to Citizenship: Opposing View," *USA Today*, December 15, 2013. www.usa today.com.
4. David Benkof, "Why Not Second-Class Citizenship for Illegal Immigrants?," *Daily Caller*, October 13, 2015. www.dailycaller.com.
5. Judy Lacey, "Illegal Immigrants Don't Deserve Favors," *Lake Havasu (AZ) News-Herald*, January 10, 2012. www.havasunews.com.
6. Quoted in Shaban, "'You Have to Live in Fear.'"

## Chapter 1: What Are the Facts?

7. American Immigration Council, "Unauthorized Immigrants Today: A Demographic Profile," August 19, 2014. www.immigrationpolicy.org.
8. Quoted in Gillen Silsby, "Why People Take the Risk of Illegal Immigration," *Futurity*, August 7, 2013. www.futurity.org.
9. Quoted in Silsby, "Why People Take the Risk of Illegal Immigration."
10. Emily Ryo, "Deciding to Cross: Norms and Economics of Unauthorized Migration," *American Sociological Review*, August 2013, p. 585.
11. Edgar Sandoval, "Texas Residents Near Mexican Border Watch Immigrants Enter U.S. Illegally Each Day," *New York Daily News*, July 14, 2014. www.nydailynews.com.
12. Sara Murray, "U.S. News: Many Here Illegally Overstayed Their Visas," *Wall Street Journal*, April 8, 2013, p. A4.
13. Jie Zong and Jeanne Batalova, "Frequently Requested Statistics on Immigrants and Immigration in the United States," *Migration Policy Institute*, April 14, 2016. www.migrationpolicy.org.

14. US Customs and Border Protection, "Immigration Inspection Program." www.cbp.gov.
15. Quoted in Catherine E. Shoichet and Madison Park, "ACLU Alleges 'Unchecked Abuse' at U.S.-Mexico Border," CNN, May 17, 2016. www.cnn.com.
16. Jim Glennon, "No Respect: Borders and Border Patrol," Police One.com, July 13, 2009. www.policeone.com.
17. US Immigration and Customs Enforcement, *ICE Enforcement and Removal Operations Report, Fiscal Year 2015*. Washington, DC: US Immigration and Customs Enforcement, 2015, p. 1.
18. Quoted in Tyche Hendricks, "U.S. Citizens Wrongly Detained, Deported by ICE," *San Francisco Chronicle*, July 27, 2009. www.sfgate.com.
19. Amnesty International, *Jailed Without Justice: Immigration Detention in the USA*, March 25, 2009. www.amnestyusa.org.
20. Jean-Claude Velasquez, "The Invisible & Voiceless: The Plight of the Undocumented Immigrant in America," Business Ethics, September 30, 2014. www.business-ethics.com.
21. Reuters, "Americans Worry That Illegal Migrants Threaten Way of Life, Economy," August 7, 2014. www.reuters.com.
22. Jeff Sessions, *Immigration Handbook for the New Republican Majority*, January 2015. www.session.senate.gov.

## Chapter 2: Should America Strengthen Disincentives to Hiring Illegal Workers?

23. Francis Wilkinson, "Why I Hire Undocumented Workers," Bloomberg View, March 12, 2014. www.bloombergview.com.
24. Quoted in *Oregonian* (Portland, OR), "Are Businesses Bad for Hiring Illegal Immigrants?," September 5, 2014. www.oregonlive.com.
25. *Oregonian* (Portland, OR), "Are Businesses Bad for Hiring Illegal Immigrants?"
26. Daniel González, "Wehirealiens.com: Vigilante or Public Service?," *Arizona Republic* (Phoenix, AZ), January 10, 2007. www.azcentral.com.
27. Quoted in González, "Wehirealiens.com."

28. Quoted in Susan Carroll, "Companies Pay Millions for Hiring Illegal Immigrants," *Houston Chronicle*, January 24, 2012. www.chron.com.
29. Jessica Vaughan, "ICE Records Reveal Steep Drop in Worksite Enforcement Since 2013," Center for Immigration Studies, June 2015. www.cis.org.
30. Barack Obama, "Remarks by the President on Comprehensive Immigration Reform," White House, January 29, 2013. www.whitehouse.gov.
31. Quoted in Julián Aguilar, "Abbott Signs Bill Mandating Use of E-Verify," *Texas Tribune*, June 10, 2105. www.texastribune.org.
32. Quoted in C-SPAN, *Washington Journal*, March 14, 2011. www.c-span.org.
33. Quoted in Congressman Lamar Smith, "Smith Introduces Legal Workforce Act Alongside Immigration Enforcement Bills," press release, February 27, 2015. http://lamarsmith.house.gov.
34. Lamar Smith, "Trust but E-Verify," *American Spectator*, October 2011, p. 8.
35. Gabriel Camacho, "The Drawbacks of E-Verify Immigration Bill," *New York Times*, March 30, 2015, p. A18.
36. Alex Nowrasteh. "The Economic Costs of E-Verify," *Federalist*, November 11, 2013. www.federalist.com.
37. Nowrasteh, "The Economic Costs of E-Verify."
38. Henrik Temp, "5 Problems with E-Verify," American Enterprise Institute, February 14, 2013. www.aei.org.
39. David Bier, "No Limits to Senate's E-Verify National ID System," *Huffington Post*, June 19, 2013. www.huffingtonpost.com.
40. Ruben Navarrette Jr., "Enforce Laws vs. Hiring Illegal Immigrants," CNN, April 3, 2009. www.cnn.com.

## Chapter 3: Should the United States Build a Wall Along the Border with Mexico?

41. Quoted in Paul Steinhauser, "Why Donald Trump's Campaign Push Is Different This Time Around," *Washington Post*, April 27, 2015. www.washingtonpost.com.
42. Quoted in Noah Bierman, "Donald Trump Says the Wall He'll Build on the Border Could Bear His Name," *Los Angeles Times*, August 15, 2015. www.latimes.com.

43. Quoted in *Huffington Post*, "Herman Cain Proposes Electrified Border Fence as Immigration Reform, Says He Was Jok-
ing," December 16, 2011. www.huffingtonpost.com.

44. Bill O'Reilly, *The O'Reilly Factor*, Fox News, July 16, 2014.
www.archive.org.

45. Kate Drew, "This Is What Trump's Border Wall Could Cost
US," CNBC, October 9, 2015. www.cnbc.com.

46. Associated Press, "Arizona Border Fence Plan Stalled After 3
Years," *USA Today*, November 6, 2013. www.usatoday.com.

47. Quoted in Tom LoBianco, "Donald Trump Promises Mexico
Will Pay for Wall," CNN, July 31, 2015. www.cnn.com.

48. Scott Eric Kaufman, "Donald Trump's Foreign-Policy Platform
Is So Catastrophically Bad That World Leaders Are Now Tak-
ing the Time to Pan It: 'It Reflects an Enormous Ignorance,'"
Salon, August 13, 2015. www.salon.com.

49. Quoted in Holly Ellyatt and Hadley Gamble, "Mexico Won't
Pay a Cent for Trump's 'Stupid Wall,'" CNBC, February 8,
2016. www.cnbc.com.

50. Boonsri Dickinson, "U.S.-Mexican Border Wall Destroying
Habitats for Endangered Animals," *HuffPost Green* (blog),
*Huffington Post*, May 25, 2011. www.huffingtonpost.com.

51. Quoted in Melissa Gaskill, "The Environmental Impact of the
U.S.-Mexico Border Wall," *Newsweek*, February 14, 2016.
www.newsweek.com.

52. Bob Ortega, "Pronghorns in Peril," *Arizona Republic* (Phoenix, AZ), January 23, 2013. www.azcentral.com.

53. Anahi Aradas, "US-Mexico Border: Efforts to Build a Virtual
Wall," BBC News, August 29, 2012. www.bbc.com.

54. Quoted in Minuteman Civil Defense Corps, "Virtual Fence Will
Fail to Deter Illegals," press release, MinutemanHQ.com, February 7, 2007. www.minutemanhq.com.

55. Quoted in Richard Finger, "The Border Fence: Horrible Deal
at Cost up to $40,000 per Illegal Immigrant Apprehended,"
*Forbes*, July 18, 2013. www.forbes.com.

56. Quoted in John Burnett, "In South Texas, Few on the Fence
over Divisive Border Wall Issue," *Morning Edition*, NPR, August 18, 2014. www.npr.org.

# Chapter 4: Should Illegal Immigrants Be Deported?

57. Quoted in Cedar Attanasio, "ICE Raids 2016: Immigration Police Round Up Central American Migrants Slated for Deportation," *Latin Times*, January 4, 2016. www.latintimes.com.

58. Quoted in Brian Bennett, "Immigration Officials Plan Increased Deportations in 2016," *Ames (IA) Tribune*, December 25, 1015. www.amestrib.com.

59. Peter Margulies et al., "*Texas v. United States*," legal brief, Cato Institute, January 7, 2015. www.cato.org.

60. Steven A. Camarota, "The Fiscal and Economic Impact of Administrative Amnesty," Center for Immigration Studies, March 17, 2015. www.cis.org.

61. Tom Camizzi, "Illegal Immigrants Need to Be Deported," *Buffalo (NY) News*, January 12, 2014. www.buffalonews.com.

62. Rasmussen Reports, "Most Voters Want to Send Latest Illegal Immigrants Home ASAP," July 17, 2014. www.rasmussen.com.

63. Martine Kalaw, "America Should Think Hard Before Deporting Undocumented Immigrants like Me," *Latino Voices* (blog), *Huffington Post*, January 19, 2016. www.huffingtonpost.com.

64. Quoted in Sam Quinones, "In Tijuana, Mexicans Deported by U.S. Struggle to Find 'Home,'" *National Geographic*, November 21, 2014. www.nationalgeographic.com.

65. Quinones, "In Tijuana, Mexicans Deported by U.S. Struggle to Find 'Home.'"

66. Quoted in Families for Freedom, "Valuing Our Families and Our Children: Child Citizen Protection Act (H.R. 182)." www.familiesforfreedom.org.

67. Ben Gitis and Laura Collins, "The Budgetary and Economic Costs of Addressing Unauthorized Immigration: Alternative Strategies," American Action Forum, March 6, 2015. www.americanactionforum.org.

68. Robert Rector and Jason Richwine, "The Fiscal Cost of Unlawful Immigrants and Amnesty to the U.S. Taxpayer," Heritage Foundation Special Report #133, May 6, 2013. www.heritage.org.

69. Rector and Richwine, "The Fiscal Cost of Unlawful Immigrants and Amnesty to the U.S. Taxpayer."

70. Bloomberg View editorial staff, "Obama's Deportation Raids Are Ugly—and Right," Bloomberg View, January 14, 2016. www.bloomberg.com.

## Chapter 5: Should the United States Employ a Path to Citizenship for Illegal Immigrants?

71. Barack Obama and Joseph Biden, "The Obama-Biden Plan," Change.org, 2008. www.change.org.

72. Quoted in NPR staff, "A Reagan Legacy: Amnesty for Illegal Immigrants," *All Things Considered*, NPR, July 4, 2010. www.npr.org.

73. Quoted in Kenneth T. Walsh, "Obama Takes to Hispanic TV to Push Immigration," *U.S. News & World Report*, July 17, 2013. www.usnews.com.

74. Quoted in White House, "Earned Citizenship." www.whitehouse.gov.

75. Quoted in Ginger Gibson, "Boehner: No Vote on Senate Immigration Bill," Politico, July 8, 2013. www.politico.com.

76. Jared Bernstein, "Path to Citizenship and Out of Poverty," Economic Policy Institute, June 29, 2006. www.epi.org.

77. Esther Yu-Hsi Lee, "Why Citizenship Is Better for America than Legal Status," Think Progress, January 31, 2014. www.thinkprogress.org.

78. Cecilia Muñoz and Gene Sperling, "The Economic Benefits of Providing a Path to Earned Citizenship," White House, August 13, 2013. www.whitehouse.gov.

79. US Senate Committee on the Budget, "Major Flaw in Gang of Eight Plan Could Cost Taxpayers Trillions," April 4, 2013. www.budget.senate.gov.

80. US Senate Committee on the Budget, "Major Flaw in Gang of Eight Plan Could Cost Taxpayers Trillions."

81. Fox News, "Republicans Estimate Immigration Bill Could Cost Taxpayers Billions, Rubio Challenges Claim," April 4, 2013. www.foxnews.com.

82. Peter Skerry, "A Path to Citizenship—or a Maze?," *Boston Globe*, February 25, 2013. www.bostonglobe.com.

83. Jeb Bush and Clint Bolick, *Immigration Wars: Forging an American Solution*. New York: Threshold, 2013, p. 43.

84. Nick Chiles, "Obama Willing to Compromise on Whether Immigration Reform Includes a Path to Citizenship," Atlanta Black Star, January 31, 2014. www.atlantablackstar.com.

85. Quoted in Chiles, "Obama Willing to Compromise on Whether Immigration Reform Includes a Path to Citizenship."

86. Quoted in Amy Chozick, "A Path to Citizenship, Hillary Clinton Says, 'Is at Its Heart a Family Issue,'" *New York Times*, May 5, 2016. www.nytimes.com.

87. Quoted in Miriam Jordan, "Many Avoid Tough Path to Citizenship," *Wall Street Journal*, March 4, 2013. www.wsj.com.

## American Immigration Control Foundation (AIC)

PO Box 525
Monterey, VA 24465
phone: (540) 468-2022
website: www.aicfoundation.com

The AIC is a nonprofit organization that advocates for reduced levels of immigration into the United States. Through its website, it disseminates news about the negative impact of illegal immigration and calls for reform that would cap all forms of immigration. AIC books, pamphlets, and videos are available on its website.

## American Immigration Council

1331 G St. NW, Suite 200
Washington, DC 20005
phone: (202) 507-7500
website: www.americanimmigrationcouncil.org

The American Immigration Council is an independent advocacy organization that promotes diversity in the United States and champions the rights of immigrants. Press releases and research reports are available to download from its website. The council's blog and list of educational programs also contain issue-related information and opinion.

## Americas Program

Cerrada de Xolalpa 7ª-3
Colonia Tortuga, Mexico
phone: 011-52-555-324-1201
website: www.cipamericas.org

Part of the US Center for International Policy, the Americas Program promotes cooperation among nations in the Western Hemisphere by addressing economic, environmental, and immigration issues. Policy briefs, reports, and editorial commentary by its members are accessible through the organization's website.

## Center for Immigration Studies (CIS)

1629 K St. NW, Suite 600
Washington, DC 20006
phone: (202) 466-8185
website: www.cis.org

The CIS is a nonpartisan think tank that researches immigration's effects on US society and the economy. The organization insists on border security and reduced levels of illegal immigration, but it does not believe such policies should endorse ill feelings toward the undocumented immigrant communities in the United States. It publishes backgrounders, member editorials, and policy testimonials on its website to share its research.

## Federation for American Immigration Reform (FAIR)

25 Massachusetts Ave. NW, Suite 330
Washington, DC 20001
phone: (877) 627-3247
website: www.fairus.org

FAIR maintains that immigration reform is needed to preserve America's economy and national well-being. For these reasons, it supports secure borders and deterring illegal immigration. FAIR produces fact sheets and policy reports about all aspects of immigration, and these as well as testimonies before Congress on immigration issues are available on its website.

## National Immigration Forum

50 F St. NW, Suite 300
Washington, DC 20001
phone: (202) 347-0040
website: www.immigrationforum.org

Formed as an immigrant rights organization, the National Immigration Forum continues its mission of supporting immigrants in the United States. On the issue of illegal immigration, the forum reaches out to lawmakers and other authorities to explain the contributions and hardships of undocumented persons. It discloses its views through fact sheets and briefs available on its website.

## US Department of Homeland Security (DHS)

Washington, DC 20528
phone: (202) 282-8000
website: www.dhs.gov

The DHS is a cabinet-level office that is chiefly responsible for protecting America from terrorism and other threats to the nation's security. Three of its dependent agencies—the USCIS, the CBP, and US Immigration and Customs Enforcement—are tasked with securing national borders and contending with legal and illegal immigration matters. DHS initiatives as well as government policy involving immigration can be found on its website.

## Books

Aviva Chomsky, *Undocumented: How Immigration Became Illegal*. Boston: Beacon, 2014.

Tanya Maria Golash-Boza, *Immigration Nation: Raids, Detentions, and Deportations in Post-9/11 America*. New York: Routledge, 2012.

Robert Lee Maril, *The Fence: National Security, Public Safety, and Illegal Immigration Along the U.S.-Mexico Border*. Lubbock: Texas Tech University Press, 2011.

Marie Friedmann Marquardt et al., *Living "Illegal": The Human Face of Unauthorized Immigration*. New York: New Press, 2013.

Terry Sterling, *Illegal: Life and Death in Arizona's Immigration War Zone*. Guilford, CT: Lyons, 2010.

## Internet Sources

American Immigration Council, "Removal Without Recourse: The Growth of Summary Deportations from the United States," April 28, 2014. http://immigrationpolicy.org/just-facts/removal-without-recourse-growth-summary-deportations-united-states.

Howard W. Foster, "Why More Immigration Is Bad for America," *The Buzz* (blog), *National Interest*, September 5, 2014. http://nationalinterest.org/blog/the-buzz/why-more-immigration-bad-america-11210.

Fox News, "Cost of Giving Illegal Immigrants Path to Citizenship Could Outweigh Fiscal Benefits," January 29, 2013. www.foxnews.com/politics/2013/01/28/cost-giving-illegal-immigrants-path-to-citizenship-could-outweigh-fiscal.html.

Diana Furchtgott-Roth, "The Economic Benefits of Immigration," Manhattan Institute for Policy Research, February 13, 2013. www.manhattan-institute.org/html/economic-benefits-immigration-5712.html.

Lourdes Medrano, "Trump's Border Wall Would Be Hard to Build—Even If Mexico Pays," *Christian Science Monitor*, April 6, 2016.

www.csmonitor.com/USA/Politics/2016/0406/Trump-s-wall
-would-be-hard-to-build-even-if-Mexico-pays-video.

Michael Oleaga, "Millennials on Immigration: Government Should
Not Deport All Immigrants from US," *Latin Post*, December 7,
2015. www.latinpost.com/articles/99961/20151207/millennials
-on-immigration-government-should-not-deport-all-immigrants
-from-us.htm.

Benjy Sarlin, "Yep, the Immigration Bill's Path to Citizenship Is the
Real Deal," Talking Points Memo, April 16, 2013. http://talking
pointsmemo.com/dc/yep-the-immigration-bill-s-path-to-citizen
ship-is-the-real-deal.

Danny Vinik, "How Much Would It Cost to Deport All Undocumented Immigrants?," *New Republic*, July 8, 2014. https://new
republic.com/article/118602/deporting-all-undocumented-immi
grants-would-cost-billions-immigration.

## Websites

**Cato Institute** (www.cato.org). The Cato Institute is a libertarian
research organization that offers opinion and testimony to policy
makers. It has a specific research group devoted to immigration
matters, and various commentaries and reports on free market
solutions to America's immigration problems are available on its
website.

**Heritage Foundation** (www.heritage.org). The Heritage Foundation is a conservative think tank. Although it offers debate on
many issues, its specific views on immigration and border security can be found in the "Immigration" section of its website.
There, its members post blog reports, backgrounders, and policy
briefs on the negative economic and social impacts of unchecked
illegal immigration.

**Pew Research Center** (www.pewhispanic.org). The Pew Research Center is an opinion poll and statistics-gathering organization that keeps track of various national issues. Its "Hispanic
Trends" section covers Americans' views on topics such as illegal
immigration and policy reform.